MW01322449

Piracy on the High Seas

Other titles in the World History Series

Auschwitz
Aztec Civilization
The Black Death
The Bombing of Pearl Harbor
Genghis Khan and the Mongol Empire
Influenza Pandemics
The Information Revolution
The Islamic Empire
The Israeli-Palestinian Conflict
Maya Civilization
Polar Explorations
The Red Scare
The Rwanda Genocide
The Scientific Revolution
The Vikings
The Women's Movement

Piracy on the High Seas

Diane Yancey

LUCENT BOOKS

A part of Gale, Cengage Learning

Detroit • New York • San Francisco • New Haven, Conn • Waterville, Maine • London

LIBRARY OF CONGRESS CATALOGING-IN-PUBLICATION DATA

Yancey, Diane.
Piracy on the high seas / by Diane Yancey.
p. cm. -- (World history)
Includes bibliographical references and index.
ISBN 978-1-4205-0679-2 (hardcover)
1. Pirates--Juvenile literature. 2. Piracy--Juvenile literature. I. Title.
G535.Y36 2012
364.16'4--dc23

2011039641

Lucent Books
27500 Drake Rd.
Farmington Hills, MI 48331

ISBN-13: 978-1-4205-0679-2
ISBN-10: 1-4205-0679-X

Printed in the United States of America
1 2 3 4 5 6 7 15 14 13 12 11

Contents

Foreword

Each year, on the first day of school, nearly every history teacher faces the task of explaining why his or her students should study history. Many reasons have been given. One is that lessons exist in the past from which contemporary society can benefit and learn. Another is that exploration of the past allows us to see the origins of our customs, ideas, and institutions. Concepts such as democracy, ethnic conflict, or even things as trivial as fashion or mores, have historical roots.

Reasons such as these impress few students, however. If anything, these explanations seem remote and dull to young minds. Yet history is anything but dull. And therein lies what is perhaps the most compelling reason for studying history: History is filled with great stories. The classic themes of literature and drama—love and sacrifice, hatred and revenge, injustice and betrayal, adversity and overcoming adversity—fill the pages of history books, feeding the imagination as well as any of the great works of fiction do.

The story of the Children's Crusade, for example, is one of the most tragic in history. In 1212 Crusader fever hit Europe. A call went out from the pope that all good Christians should journey to Jerusalem to drive out the hated Muslims and return the city to Christian control. Heeding the call, thousands of children made the journey. Parents bravely allowed many children to go, and entire communities were inspired by the faith of these small Crusaders. Unfortunately, many boarded ships were captained by slave traders, who enthusiastically sold the children into slavery as soon as they arrived at their destination. Thousands died from disease, exposure, and starvation on the long march across Europe to the Mediterranean Sea. Others perished at sea.

Another story, from a modern and more familiar place, offers a soul-wrenching view of personal humiliation but also the ability to rise above it. Hatsuye Egami was one of 110,000 Japanese Americans sent to internment camps during World War II. "Since yesterday we Japanese have ceased to be human beings," he wrote in his diary. "We are numbers. We are no longer Egamis, but the number 23324. A tag with that number is on every trunk, suitcase and bag. Tags, also, on our breasts." Despite such dehumanizing treatment, most internees worked hard to control their bitterness. They created workable communities inside the camps and demonstrated again and again their loyalty as Americans.

These are but two of the many stories from history that can be found in the pages of the Lucent Books World History series. All World History titles rely on sound research and verifiable evidence, and all give students a clear sense of time, place, and chronology through maps and timelines as well as text.

All titles include a wide range of authoritative perspectives that demonstrate the complexity of historical interpretation and sharpen the reader's critical thinking skills. Formally documented quotations and annotated bibliographies enable students to locate and evaluate sources, often instantaneously via the Internet, and serve as valuable tools for further research and debate.

Finally, Lucent's World History titles present rousing good stories, featuring vivid primary source quotations drawn from unique, sometimes obscure sources such as diaries, public records, and contemporary chronicles. In this way, the voices of participants and witnesses as well as important biographers and historians bring the study of history to life. As we are caught up in the lives of others, we are reminded that we too are characters in the ongoing human saga, and we are better prepared for our own roles.

Important Dates

5000 B.C. Earliest-known seafaring vessel.

1400 B.C. First-known pirates begin raiding in the Mediterranean Sea.

1333 B.C. King Tutankhamun begins rule in Egypt.

1200 B.C. Thracian pirates plunder the Greek coast.

75 B.C. Julius Caesar is captured by Cilician pirates.

6 B.C. The approximate birth date of Jesus Christ.

A.D. 395 The end of the Roman Empire.

570 The Prophet Muhammad, founder of Islam, is born.

589 The first recorded pirate attack in the South China Sea.

1100 Wokou pirates sail out of Japan.

1150 The Chinese develop rockets.

1275 The explorer Marco Polo arrives in Kublai Khan's court in China.

1440 Johannes Gutenberg invents the printing press.

1453 The Ottomans capture Constantinople, the capital of Turkey, marking the end of the Roman Empire.

1492 Christopher Columbus "discovers" the New World.

1564 William Shakespeare is born.

1570 Francis Drake is commissioned as a privateer by Elizabeth I of England.

1625 The earliest documented attack by Barbary pirates.

1650 The Golden Age of Piracy begins.

1698 Privateer Kanhoji Angre claims the Maratha fort of Vijaydurg as his first pirate base.

1730 The Golden Age of Piracy ends.

1776 America declares independence from Britain.

1794 The U.S. Navy is created due to the threat from Barbary pirates.

B.C. 1300 — AD. 1000 — 1300 — 1500 — 1700

of the Period

1801
The First Barbary War begins.

1807
Madame Zheng assumes control of her husband's pirate empire.

1815
The Second Barbary War begins.

1862
The American Civil War begins.

1914
World War I begins.

1939
World War II begins.

1965
The first Americans are killed in the Vietnam War.

1991
The government of Somalia collapses.

2001
Terrorists destroy the World Trade Center.

2004
The Malacca Strait Patrols is formed to fight piracy.

1800 | 1850 | 1900 | 1950 | 2000

2006
The International Maritime Bureau reports that ten vessels were attacked by Somali pirates.

2007
The United Nations Security Council votes to allow countries to send warships into Somali waters to handle pirates.

2009
The *Maersk Alabama* becomes the first American vessel to be hijacked by pirates since the early 1800s.

2010
The United States tries five Somali pirates in federal court; they are given life sentences.

2011
Four Americans on board the *Quest* are killed by Somali pirates.

Introduction

Piracy: Fact and Fantasy

Jean and Scott Adam were a couple of ordinary Americans, happy to be spending their retirement years sailing around the world in their small yacht, the *Quest*. They enjoyed life at sea and, as part of a personal missionary effort, distributed Bibles to schools and churches in places like Alaska, Mexico, and the Cook Islands in the South Pacific.

On February 1, 2011, with friends Robert Riggle and Phyllis Macay, the Adams left Mumbai, India, and crossed the Arabian Sea, headed toward Oman on the southern coast of the Arabian Peninsula. The area was notorious for attacks by Somali pirates—desperate young men who usually preyed on cargo ships—but the Adams were experienced yachters and believed they were relatively safe.

They were mistaken. Before they could reach Oman, nineteen armed pirates stopped them and boarded the yacht. An SOS distress call from the *Quest* alerted nearby U.S. warships to the hijacking, and several raced to the rescue. For four days they shadowed the *Quest* and tried to negotiate with the pirates to release the captives. On February 22, however, something went wrong. The sound of shots on board the yacht caused naval forces to attack the pirates. Several were killed and the rest were taken captive, but it was too late to save the Americans, who had been shot to death. "Everybody thinks, 'It's not going to happen to me, hundreds of boats get through there,'"[1] said a friend of the Adams, Vicky Mullen.

This incident is just one of the latest examples of how maritime piracy—piracy on the high seas—has been and continues to be a serious problem. Journalist Charlotte Sector writes, "Skull and crossbones buccaneers have resurfaced with 'Terminator'-style tactics, shining a spotlight on an age-old crime."[2]

An Ancient Problem

There has been piracy on the high seas since ships first began to sail the oceans. The Vedas, ancient Indian texts dating from 2000 to 1100 B.C., speak of pirate attacks that took place early in that country's history. In the twelfth and thirteenth centuries B.C, seafaring raiders known as the Sea Peoples plundered Egyptian ships in the Middle East.

No matter when or where it occurs, maritime piracy is defined as robbery and/or criminal acts of violence committed on any major body of water and the land edging that water. It can involve taking cargo, hijacking an entire ship, or holding passengers for ransom, and it always happens for reasons of personal profit. This is what makes piracy different from maritime terrorism, which is committed for political reasons. The bombing of the USS *Cole* on October 12, 2000, for instance, is an example of maritime terrorism. In that incident nothing was stolen, but seventeen sailors were killed, and the terrorist group al-Qaeda claimed responsibility for the attack.

Despite the fact that piracy is a violent act, it is often seen as being part of an adventurous, fascinating, and romantic way of life. Early pirates were feared, but they were also often secretly admired. They were considered brave and strong. They dared to ignore the laws of polite society. Most importantly, pirates enjoyed total freedom. They traveled around the world in control of their own lives. In the words of historian Peter Earle, they "sailed their beautiful ships through beautiful tropical seas before running down a prize [ship] and swinging aboard with astonishing agility and ferocity."[3]

Deadly Statistics

Anyone who has seen Walt Disney's *Peter Pan* or the *Pirates of the Caribbean* movies may have gotten the impression that pirates are romantic and relatively harmless individuals from an earlier era. The sobering statistics, published by the International Maritime Bureau, prove otherwise.

Here is the deadly reality for the first three months of 2011 alone:

- 142 pirate attacks worldwide
- 18 vessels seized by pirates
- 344 crew members captured and held hostage
- 34 crew members injured
- 7 crew members murdered

Romance and Practicality

In the nineteenth and twentieth centuries, novels and Hollywood movies often emphasized the romance of piracy. In books like Robert Louis Stevenson's *Treasure Island*, pirates buried chests of treasure and carried parrots on their shoulders. Hollywood movies like *Captain Blood* and *Swashbuckler* portrayed the outlaws as handsome, well mannered, and generous to females and the poor. Author James Robert Parrish writes of the fictional movie pirate, "[He was] a man fighting for the right in a world that does not understand the right as he sees it."[4]

Much about these fictional accounts was inaccurate, however. Most real pirates were not well mannered or generous. They usually became outlaws because they were out of work, poor, and greedy. They broke laws and often killed people while carrying out attacks. Unlike their fictional counterparts, many pirates were mean and cruel. Author Edward E. Leslie writes of one pirate, Edward Low, "The psychopath's history . . . is filled with mutilations, disembowelings, decapitations, and slaughter."[5]

Fictional pirates were also portrayed as independent adventurers, but piracy was frequently big business. A monarch or corrupt government official who wanted to make money or undermine a rival country's economy often made it financially worthwhile for men to go into piracy. Queen Elizabeth I supported Francis Drake in attacking and stealing from Spanish ships in the 1570s. Royal Governor of Pennsylvania William

This ancient Roman mosaic depicting a struggle against pirates shows that piracy has been a problem for centuries.

Fact and Fiction

Novelists and film producers mix fact and fiction when creating their books and movies. In his book Under the Black Flag, *author David Cordingly points out:*

More than seventy films have been made about pirates, buccaneers and corsairs. While some film directors and producers have gone to considerable lengths to build pirate ships, stage elaborate sea battles, and film in appropriate locations . . . it is curious how few of the films follow the historical events with any accuracy. Most are based on works of fiction, or plunder the histories of the real pirates with a . . . disregard for the facts. There is nothing wrong with this. . . . But the fact remains that the lives of some of the real pirates and the men who hunted them down are as fascinating and as full of drama as any of the works of fiction.

David Cordingly. *Under the Black Flag: The Romance and the Reality of Life Among the Pirates*. New York: Random House, 1995, p. 177.

Markham and Royal Governor of New York Benjamin Fletcher encouraged and financially backed pirates in America in the 1690s. Backing pirates was technically illegal for monarchs, but it was less expensive and less politically risky than waging a war.

Requirements for Piracy

In order for piracy to take place, many elements had to be present, in addition to the participation of lawless and corrupt men. First, the pirates needed to be able to count on maritime trade routes through which merchant ships regularly passed. There had to be places on those routes that were beyond the reach of the law; where no nearby law enforcement ships could interfere with a pirate's attack. Pirates also needed hideouts—bays, coves, and rivers—and trading posts where they could lie low, resupply their ships, and dispose of stolen goods.

Those ideal conditions existed in the Mediterranean and the Caribbean in early times, and they exist in Somalia and Southeast Asia today. Piracy was a problem in the past, and it is a growing problem in the modern world. Although pirates have given up sailing ships for modern motorboats and cutlasses for automatic weapons, they remain ruthless and lawless, ready to steal treasure and take lives. "Piracy is not a thing of the past, a romanticized form of crime from the pages of history," says pirate expert Angus Konstam. "It still happens every day, and the victims don't always live to tell the tale."[6]

Chapter One

The Barbary Pirates

Robbery on the high seas dates back to ancient times and has its roots in greed, financial need, and the love of adventure. Humans have long depended on the sea to make a living, and daring men in ships or boats were always willing to take the law into their own hands and risk their lives to gain wealth. Books and movies have romanticized their lives, but pirates were seldom charming characters like Captain Jack Sparrow in Disney's *Pirates of the Caribbean*.

In fact, pirates were no-nonsense marauders, bent on pillage and plunder. They commonly fell into two categories based on their motives for stealing. One pirate group consisted of greedy outlaws who were loyal to no man, attacked ships of any country, and kept stolen goods for themselves. Over time, these types of pirates were called sea thieves, sea rovers, freebooters, *flibustiers*, and swashbucklers. Pirate expert Cindy Vallar explains where some of these names came from:

> In the 1800s, authors translated the Dutch word *vrijbuiter* into freebooter, a person who searched for ill-gotten gains. . . . French authors called Caribbean pirates *flibustiers*. When [the word] swashbuckler first appeared in writings of the 16th century, it referred to someone who made a loud noise by striking his sword against his shield. Today the word often refers to pirates or movies about them.[7]

A second group of pirates was known as privateers. They were loyal to their country of choice and stole for their sponsor, who could be a wealthy merchant or a king or queen. They carried official letters of marque, which entitled them to attack and loot the ships of enemy countries. Their efforts enhanced weak royal navies and helped fill royal treasuries. They gave their loot to the sponsor and received a generous portion as a reward for their services. Privateers had a semi-legal status in the world, and their countrymen saw them as heroes. To their enemies, of course, they were viewed as outlaws.

Pirate Hot Spot

Both types of pirates looted in the Mediterranean Sea over the centuries. The Thracians, some of the earliest known pirates, who plundered the Greek coast in the thirteenth century B.C. from what is now southern Turkey, troubled the

Caesar and the Pirates

One of the earliest pirate kidnappings took place in 75 B.C. Roman statesman Julius Caesar was captured by pirates on the Aegean Sea while traveling from Italy to Rhodes. The pirates held him for ransom, demanding twenty talents for his release. A talent was any amount of precious metal weighing 71 pounds (32.3kg). Offended that they did not recognize his importance, Caesar informed them he was worth fifty talents and sent his servants to raise that amount. While waiting for the ransom to be paid, he grew friendly with his captors. He read poems and speeches to them and laughingly threatened to have them all hanged because they did not appreciate his readings.

The pirates did not take him seriously, but after the ransom was paid and he was freed, Caesar raised a small fleet of ships and went after the outlaws. He captured them with ease, then put them to death, just as he had promised. Greek historian Plutarch wrote, "He took the pirates out of prison and crucified the lot of them, just as he had often told them he would do when he was on the island and they imagined that he was joking."

Quoted in Angus Konstam. *Piracy: The Complete History*. New York: Osprey, 2008, p. 19.

Julius Caesar was kidnapped by pirates, but he eventually crucified them for their criminal activities in 75 B.C.

area beginning in the second century B.C. Illyrian tribes who lived in what is now Albania and Montenegro in the Western Balkans were so dangerous in 230 B.C. that the Roman Empire went to war to wipe them out. And Turkish privateers from the Ottoman Empire plagued the region from the sixteenth to the nineteenth centuries.

There were many reasons that the Mediterranean was a hot spot of piracy. Mountains prevented easy overland passage between Asia and Europe, so the main lines of communication and trade were by sea. Merchant ships that passed to and fro on the Mediterranean usually followed established routes that were close to the coast. That made it relatively easy for sea thieves to plan and carry out attacks. As geographer Ellen Churchill Semple writes, "The pirate was the robber of the sea highways: and the highways of the Mediterranean were well-defined and well-traveled."[8]

While ships filled with valuable cargo sailed on the Mediterranean, people living on its coastline were poor. Their land was barren and rocky. It could not support large-scale farming, so any villages that developed were small. Inhabitants relied on fishing for income, but when fishing was bad, they had to look for other ways to make a living. Most able-bodied men had boats and were at home on the sea, and so, for some, piracy became a source of income that gave them more wealth than fishing alone.

Expansion of Islam

Piracy in the Mediterranean was not just motivated by money. It was also motivated by religious differences. The Roman Empire—the most powerful political force in Europe between 27 B.C. and A.D. 395—adopted Christianity as its official religion in A.D. 380. During the early Middle Ages (A.D. 500 to 1000), most of the people of Europe and the area around the Mediterranean were Christians.

But the Roman Empire did not last forever. As its power began waning, Turkish influence grew in the Mediterranean. The Turks originated in Asia and migrated westward beginning in the eleventh century, bringing the Islamic religion with them. The powerful Ottoman Empire was established in 1265, and by the sixteenth and seventeenth centuries, it encompassed much of southeastern Europe, western Asia, and northern Africa. The Ottomans were Muslim, and because of differing religious beliefs and a desire to expand their empire, they were often in conflict with the Roman Empire.

Muslim privateers, also known as corsairs, helped carry out Ottoman dreams of conquest. They captured merchant ships from countries such as Spain, stealing the treasure and holding the ship and crew for ransom. Their activities were considered lawful to other Muslims because their attacks were against those of a different faith, who were seen as God's enemies.

Righteousness and Profit

Corsair activity was sponsored by local government leaders in North Africa. North Africa was also known as the Barbary Coast, after the Berber tribespeople who originally lived there. During the

This fourteenth-century illustration depicts a joint English and French naval expedition setting out in 1390 to subdue African corsairs who preyed on ships in the Mediterranean.

reign of the Ottoman Empire, it was divided into states called the Regency of Algiers, Tunis, Tripolitania, and the kingdom of Morocco (present-day Algeria, Tunisia, Libya, and Morocco). Rulers of these states gave their allegiance to the Ottoman leader, or sultan, but were essentially independent. Sometimes they were even former pirates who had captured a region and continued to send their confederates out to plunder enemy shipping.

Local merchants and wealthy businessmen also supported corsair activity, because they believed that it was a good way to make a profit and please God at the same time. They gave the pirates ships and supplies, and at the end of a raid, they received a share of the treasure that had been taken. An additional 10 percent of any profits went to the supporting government. As historian Peter Earle writes, "[This kind of piracy was] a very attractive investment since it was likely to satisfy a man's desire for piety [righteousness] and profit at one and the same time."[9]

Muslim corsairs were not the only ones who fought for their faith in the Mediterranean. Maltese corsairs were Catholic privateers authorized by the Knights of St. John. The knights were a Christian military order who lived on the island of Malta in the middle of the

Mediterranean. Although small in number, the Maltese corsairs were fearless men who had the reputation of attacking and overcoming huge fleets of Muslim ships. In the words of Earle, they were "driven by a desire for profit . . . but also driven by religious zeal and a lust for adventure and glory."[10] Although the pirates of Barbary and Malta were enemies of each other, they were, in fact, similar to one another. They were businesslike, organized, motivated, and very determined to defeat the enemies of their faiths.

Convoys of Galleys

While Christian corsairs called Malta their home, the Barbary corsairs had their bases in the port of Algiers and the Moroccan port of Salé. Both were walled cities with natural harbors that provided shelter for ships. Both served as excellent home bases from which to launch attacks. Setting out from these harbors, the corsairs preyed on vessels in the western Mediterranean as well as on ships sailing around Africa on their way to Asia.

The corsairs often traveled in convoys (groups of ships), and their ships of choice were galleys—light, narrow vessels that could be easily maneuvered in shallow water. Galleys sometimes had triangular sails, but they were propelled by dozens of men—usually slaves—who sat on benches in tiers and pulled long oars in unison. In the words of former galley slave Jean Marteille de Bernac, "Think of six men chained to a bench, naked as when they were born, . . . holding an immensely heavy oar, bending forwards to the stern with arms at full reach to clear the backs of the rowers in front."[11]

The rest of the crew was made up of a collection of renegade men from all countries around the Mediterranean. These included janissaries—soldiers from the Ottoman military who had been recruited by promises of riches. Earle writes, "These turbaned warriors in their flowing robes served under their own aga [leader] and played little or no part in the sailing of the ship, sitting patiently smoking opium or tobacco until that moment of glory when . . . they swarmed over the sides of a prize."[12]

"Wild-Looking Men with Turbans"

While on the hunt for victims, corsairs disguised their galleys as merchant ships. They covered their guns. Instead of flying the flag of their home country, they flew a false flag as they approached their victim. Then, when they were close enough, they fired off their cannons and, if necessary, smashed into the other ship with a ram mounted on the bow—or front—of their vessel. Immediately after, a large boarding party swept onto the merchant ship, screaming and shouting curses, waving muskets, swords, pikes (sharp blades mounted on staffs), and knives. The surprise and terror of the attack was usually enough to cause the merchant ship to surrender quickly. If not, the pirates attacked with their weapons until the crew was overpowered.

Miserable Captives

Individuals captured by Barbary corsairs were made slaves for life unless someone purchased their freedom. As Angus Konstam writes in Piracy: The Complete History, *a few organizations were formed to do this.*

The only hope for many of the poorer captives was that some Christian religious order would buy their freedom. One of these groups—the Redemptionists—organized the purchase and freedom of some 15,500 Christian slaves of all nationalities between 1575 and 1769. Another Catholic organization called the Lazarists were equally successful. Sometimes governments took a hand in the business of raising money. For example, in 1643, seven women petitioned the English Parliament to allow churches to take up collections because "Their husbands and others were taken by Turkish pirates, carried to Algiers, and there now remain in miserable captivity, having great fines imposed on them for their ransoms."

Angus Konstam. *Piracy: The Complete History*. New York: Osprey, 2008, p. 92.

Once a ship was captured, it was taken back to land, where the cargo was unloaded and the crew held for ransom or sold as slaves. The use of slave labor was common in the Ottoman Empire, and it is estimated that between 1 million and 1.25 million non-Muslim people around the Mediterranean were enslaved by corsairs between A.D. 1530 and 1780. The only way captured crew members could hope to escape such treatment was to be ransomed or to convert to Islam.

Pirates also found victims for the slave markets from villages along the Mediterranean coastline. This caused enormous fear because no one could tell when there would be a raid on their area, with men, women, and children being kidnapped. The corsairs were so feared that many coastal inhabitants moved inland, leaving long stretches of coast in Spain and Italy almost completely abandoned. Tales of their actions survived in the form of terrifying legends. Earle writes, "Folklore reflects fears of wild-looking men with turbans and long knives who burst forth out of the mist and drag innocent families away to a lifetime of slavery."[13]

Corsair Heroes

There were hundreds of Barbary corsairs, but none were as renowned as the Barbarossa brothers, famous for their red hair and beards. (*Barbarossa* means "red beard" in Italian). Oruc (or Uruj) and Hizir Barbarossa were born in Greece in the 1470s and were sailors before they became pirates. Once they took to pirating, they were so clever and daring that they became the most successful corsairs of the Barbary Coast, with hundreds of men joining their pirate convoy.

Because Oruc was older, he assumed command of the brothers' first convoy, which harassed Spanish outposts on the North African coast and even led raids against settlements on the Spanish coast. In 1516, while fighting off a Spanish attack on Algiers, Oruc took the opportunity to seize the city from its ruler and declared himself sultan of Algiers. He then gave up his title and swore loyalty to the Ottomans in return for their help in beating back the Spanish. For his act of loyalty, he was appointed governor general of the western Mediterranean by Ottoman sultan Selim I. Konstam notes that this made him "de facto [in fact] ruler of the Barbary coast."[14]

Despite his skill and experience, Oruc was killed while fighting a fleet of galleys sent by Holy Roman Emperor Charles V in 1518. During his career as a pirate, the Barbarossa brother had proved a sizable threat to the Holy Roman Empire. Authors Stanley Lane-Poole and James Douglas Jerrold Kelley write, "He resided in Barbary fourteen years, during which time the harms he did to the Christians are inexpressible."[15]

Master of the Mediterranean

With Oruc's death, Hizir Barbarossa, also known as Kheyr-ed-din, took over his older brother's position as governor general and continued attacking ships, plundering coastlines, and capturing slaves off the southern coast of France, the Balearic Islands, and Spain. Lane-Poole and Kelley write:

> The mantle of Uruj [Oruc] had fallen upon worthy shoulders. The elder brother possessed . . . matchless qualities for deeds of derring-do [daring]; to lead a storming party, board a galleon,—cut and thrust and "have at you"—he had no equal: but Kheyr-ed-din [Hizir], with like courage and determination, was gifted with prudent and statesmanlike intelligence, which led him to greater enterprises.[16]

Hizir became known as master of the Mediterranean and the scourge of Christendom for the vessels he captured and the slaves he took. Lane-Poole and Kelley write, "His fleet increased month by month, til he had thirty-six of his own galliots [small galleys] perpetually on the cruise in the summer season; his prizes were innumerable."[17] The privateer was able to defeat Charles V's navy, which had come to put down the corsairs in 1538. The defeat secured the eastern Mediterranean for the Ottomans for the next thirty years.

As he grew older, Hizir was a prominent figure of the sultan's court in Constantinople. He remained there until his death in 1546. He is buried in Istanbul (formerly Constantinople), Turkey, where his statue stands today near the Turkish Naval Museum.

Oruc (left) and Hizir Barbarossa carved out a corsair empire in North Africa and became masters of the Mediterranean in the early sixteenth century.

Turning Turk

Corsairs who came from Greece, Turkey, and Albania were not the only pirates who looted the Mediterranean. English pirates and privateers such as Richard Bishop and Henry Mainwaring also entered the ranks of the Barbary pirates beginning in the early 1600s. They were motivated by greed and sometimes by the need to escape their home countries because they had broken the law.

Those Europeans who gave up their original roots and loyalties to adopt a life of piracy in the Mediterranean were said to have "turned Turk." Some of them even converted to Islam, like Dutch-born seaman Zymen Danseker (although he practiced Christianity in secret), and took Middle Eastern names. For instance, Danseker was also known as Simon Reis or Deli-Reis (Captain Crazy) for his many daring exploits. He was also remembered for teaching Algerian pirates European sailing skills needed to sail out into the Atlantic Ocean, a distance that few had successfully navigated before.

Another European who became a Mediterranean pirate was Dutch-born sailor Jan Janzoon van Haarlem, who was captured by Barbary corsairs and taken to Algiers as a captive in 1618. Changing his allegiance to the corsairs, Janzoon became known as Murat Reis and sailed for a time with Danseker and a Dutch corsair named De Veenboer (Sulayman Reis). He then led a dread band of pirates known as the Salee Rovers, who operated from the stronghold of Salé. While sailing off the coast of Tunis in 1635, Janzoon was captured by members of the Knights of Malta and spent five years in a dungeon, where he was mistreated and tortured. He escaped in 1640 and returned to Morocco, where he retired from piracy and lived out his life in comfort.

Captain Jack Ward

One of the most notorious European pirates in the Mediterranean was an Englishman known as Captain Jack Ward, or Yusef Reis. In the words of Sir Henry Wotton, the English ambassador to Venice, Italy, in 1607, "Ward, so well-known in this port for the damage he has done, is beyond a doubt the greatest scoundrel that ever sailed from England."[18]

Little is known of Ward's early life, but around the year 1603 he was forced to join the Royal Navy against his will. After two weeks he deserted, recruited a ship and crew, and sailed to Tunis, where he turned to piracy. He was both talented and lucky; each ship he captured proved more valuable than the

A Thorough "Salt"

Not all famous corsairs looked like the pirates of legend. Rather than being tall and sinister, Captain Jack Ward was short and stout. His personality made up for his lack of size, however. An English sailor described him in 1608: "[He was] very short with little hair, and that quite white, bald in front; swarthy face and beard. Speaks little and almost always swearing. Drunk from morn till night. . . . The habits of a thorough salt [sailor]."

Quoted in Peter Earle. *The Pirate Wars*. New York: Thomas Dunne, 2003, p. 29.

last. He ended up a wealthy man but was unable to return to England because of his lawlessness, so he converted to Islam and settled in Tunis. There he built a palace with his riches. He died of the plague in 1622.

In addition to his notorious reputation, Ward gained fame for introducing the corsairs to square-masted sailing ships, which were common in Europe. Square-masted ships were generally faster and more stable than galleys and allowed the pirates to travel greater distances into the ocean. Authors Lane-Poole and Kelley noted another benefit: "A long cruise is impossible in a galley, where you have some hundreds of rowers to feed, and where each pound of biscuit adds to the labor of motion; but sails have no mouths and can carry along a great weight of provisions without getting tired. . . . So sails triumphed over oars."[19]

Demands for Tribute

With the latest in European sailing innovation and the powerful backing of the Ottoman Empire, the Barbary corsairs were virtually uncontrollable. European powers such as Britain, France, Spain, and Netherlands might have cooperated to eradicate them, but these countries were political and commercial rivals. So if Spanish ships were attacked, the British were happy, and vice versa. With no good solution to the problem, a compromise was finally reached. Countries like Britain agreed to pay an annual sum of money to each Barbary Coast ruler. In return, that ruler's corsairs would not attack that country's ships. These agreements were irritating and embarrassing for powerful countries because they were forced to submit to the outlaw pirates. Nevertheless, most countries paid the tribute.

The United States at first followed the example of the European countries. Before gaining independence from England, the colonies had been protected under Britain's pact with the pirates. During the Revolutionary War, American ships relied on the 1778 Treaty of Alliance with France, which required that France protect them. That alliance ended in 1783, however. U.S. officials then negotiated a treaty with the bey of Morocco in 1786, but pirates from Algiers and other provinces still attacked and took hostages. In 1795 alone, the United States paid nearly $1 million to ransom 115 sailors who had been taken by Algerian pirates.

When Thomas Jefferson became president in 1801, he refused a demand for increased tribute from the bey of Tripoli. Tripoli responded by declaring war on the United States. Jefferson informed Congress in his first annual message on December 8, 1801: "Tripoli, the least considerable of the Barbary States, . . . has permitted itself to denounce war, on our failure to comply before a given day. The style of the demand admitted but one answer. I sent a small squadron of frigates [warships] into the Mediterranean . . . with orders to protect our commerce."[20] The announcement marked the start of the First Barbary War.

The Barbary Wars

The First Barbary War, between the United States and Tripoli, lasted from 1801 to 1805. During the war, the United States was successful in defeating Tripoli and raised the U.S. flag in victory on foreign soil for the first time.

The war did not solve the problem of pirate activity in the Mediterranean, however. Algerian privateers in particular continued to capture American ships and hold seamen hostage until ransom was paid. Thus, in 1815 the United States once again responded to the attacks in what became known as the Second Barbary War. This short struggle, which lasted from March to July 1815, eventually led to treaties that ended all tribute payments by the United States to the Barbary pirates.

Beginning in 1816 other European nations also began to resist the demands of the Barbary pirates. With faster ships and increasingly powerful navies, they were better able to win battles in the Mediterranean. Konstam writes, "The

Barbary corsairs attack a Spanish vessel. Many countries chose to pay tribute to the corsairs to leave their ships alone, rather than to go to war against them.

An American fleet bombards Tripoli in 1804. The United States won the war, but Algerian pirates continued to raid U.S. ships until a second war stopped tribute practices in 1815.

long history of . . . piracy ended more with a whimper than a bang, the result of a changing world and the growing importance of military technology."[21] France gained control of Algiers and Tunis and made them colonies in 1830 and 1881 respectively, while Italy assumed control of Tripoli in 1911.

While the corsairs were defeated in the Mediterranean, other pirates and privateers were still at large in other parts of the world, particularly in the Caribbean Sea. Whether they were called buccaneers or roundsmen, these men (and sometimes women) from Britain, France, and Netherlands spent years plundering the New World and gained renown for doing so. Earle writes, "The pirates of the Americas, who flourished from the 1650s to the 1720s, were . . . the only pirates in history to exhibit those characteristics which we expect 'real' pirates to have. They . . . created the modern conception of the pirate."[22]

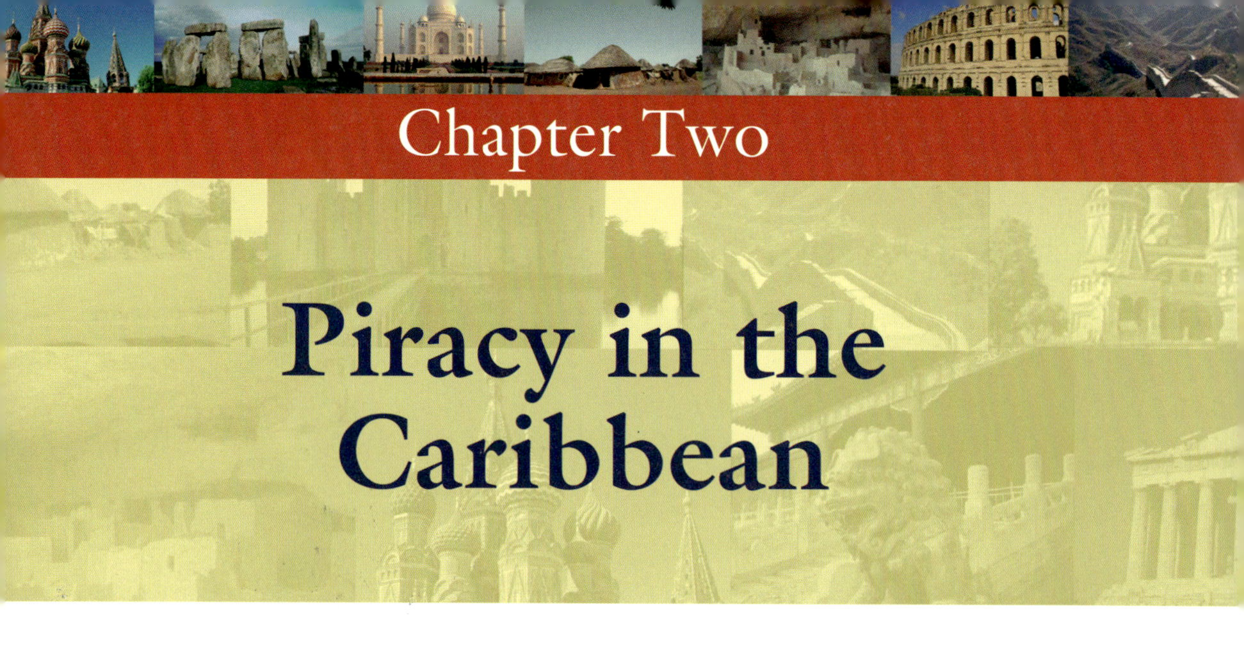

Chapter Two

Piracy in the Caribbean

The Caribbean Sea with its countless islands and miles of coastlines was a popular spot for pirates from the 1500s to the early 1800s. Known as the Spanish Main because most of the land in the region had been claimed by Spain, it had all the requirements for maritime marauding. It was far from major powers with large navies. It was part of a well-traveled maritime route. It also had plenty of places where pirates could hide and set up strongholds.

The Caribbean had come under Spanish influence when Christopher Columbus made his voyages to the New World beginning in 1492. In 1521 Spanish explorer Hernán Cortés conquered the Aztec Empire in Mexico and began sending treasure that included exotic animals, enameled gold and jade ornaments, emeralds, pearls, works of art, and mosaic masks back to his country. The rest of Europe learned of those riches when, in 1522, French privateer Jean Fleury captured Spanish ships that were carrying treasure. Author Rene Chartrand writes, "The news spread like wildfire: the fabulous wealth of the Spanish 'Indies' was soon the envy of all Europe."[23]

French Privateers

The Spanish Main was a source of enormous wealth for Spain for many years. That wealth created jealousy among other European rulers who wanted to take part in trade and colonization in the New World. Spain, however, was determined to keep the land and riches for itself. As a result, Britain, Netherlands, France, and Portugal began hiring privateers to attack Spanish ships and landholdings and to steal treasure.

Some of the first privateers to attack Spanish ships were French, including Fleury and François Le Clerc. It is not known exactly when either man began his pirating career, but by 1553 Le Clerc had assumed overall command of seven pirate craft and three royal vessels and was leading major raids against the Spanish, using the island of Saint Lucia as his home base.

Jacques Le Sores, nicknamed the Exterminating Angel, was a lesser-known French privateer who sailed with Le Clerc. A member of the Protestant faith, Le Sores hated Catholics and made a practice of setting fire to Catholic churches and chapels, with sometimes disastrous effects. One of his attacks resulted in the burning of Havana, Cuba, in 1555.

"My Pirate"

English privateers also sailed in the Caribbean. They were motivated by a desire for loot, but also by a hatred of the Spanish, with whom Britain was at war until the Treaty of London was signed in 1603. The most famous privateer was Sir Francis Drake, whom Queen Elizabeth I called "my pirate."[24] Commissioned by the queen in 1570, Drake spent seven years stealing from Spanish ships and Spanish settlements in the Caribbean. He was such a threat that Spain's king Philip II was said to have offered a reward of twenty thousand ducats (about $2 million in today's money) for his capture or death.

Drake's piracy extended outside of the Caribbean as well. In 1577 he was secretly commissioned by Elizabeth to undertake an expedition against the Spanish colonies on the Pacific coast of North America. He sailed with five ships, but by the time he rounded the tip of South America and reached the Pacific Ocean in October 1578, only one, a galleon (a large, multi-deck sailing ship) named the *Golden Hind*, remained. He continued up the coast, plundering ships along the way. From one vessel alone, the *Nuestra Señora de la Concepción*, he was able to take silver and gold worth at least $72 million in today's dollars. It was one of the most profitable pirate attacks in history. After successfully claiming a portion of California for the

Commissioned by Queen Elizabeth I to serve as a privateer, Sir Francis Drake spent seven years stealing Spanish ships and attacking Spanish settlements in the Caribbean.

queen, Drake continued homeward across the Pacific, making multiple stops as he went, and arriving in Plymouth, England, in July 1580.

Drake continued his seafaring career, but on a trip to the Caribbean in 1596, he developed dysentery and died. He was buried at sea off the coast of Panama in a lead coffin, which has never been found.

The *Boucaniers*

Despite Spanish opposition, countries like Britain, France, and Netherlands established colonies in the Spanish Main as well. The British colonized Bermuda in 1612 and Jamaica in 1655. The Dutch took over the islands known as the Dutch West Indies (Aruba, St. Croix, St. Martin, and others) beginning in the 1620s.

French colonization began in 1625 on the island of Hispaniola (now Haiti and the Dominican Republic), which was wild and undeveloped. The Spanish had unsuccessfully tried ranching there, and herds of semi-wild cattle still roamed at large. These cattle became a source of food for the colonists, who survived by smoking meat over a *boucane,* or wooden frame. These men became known as *boucaniers*—and later, buccaneers. Angus Konstam writes:

> They lived, worked and slept in rough leather hunting shirts or working clothes, coarse homespun shirts, and boots made out of pigskin. Animal fat was smeared over the skin to repel insects. . . . These men roamed the hills, rounding up wild cattle. . . . They operated in small groups, developing their own complex codes of behavior which would later develop into the buccaneering codes so beloved of pirate fiction.[25]

In this lawless atmosphere, the wild French buccaneers branched out into smuggling and piracy to make a living. They were joined by former slaves, indentured servants, and outlaws from America and other parts of the Caribbean. They were also joined by men who had served in the British Royal Navy. From the 1600s to the 1800s, England could impress any man it wanted and force him to serve on a merchant ship or in the navy. The service was incredibly hard, the wages were low, and the captain of a ship had absolute power. Life was restrictive, and crewmen could be punished by whipping for the least offense. To these men, being a pirate was a vast improvement in lifestyle, as pirate Bartholomew Roberts testified: "In an honest Service there is thin Commons [limited food], low Wages, and hard Labour; in this [being a pirate], Plenty and Satiety [satisfaction], Pleasure and Ease, Liberty and Power. . . . A merry Life and a short one, shall be my Motto."[26]

Pirates of Tortuga

The activities of the buccaneers between 1650 and 1680 marked the first phase of the Golden Age of Piracy. Despite Spain's attempts to end piracy, the practice flourished during these years. When authorities tried to clear Hispaniola of the

Black Pirates on the Spanish Main

Better accounts of pirates exist for the Golden Age of Piracy than in any earlier period, but there are no records of the number of black pirates who sailed the Spanish Main. Editor Cindy Vallar explains:

Some estimate that nearly 5,000 pirates hunted prey between 1715 and 1726. Of that number, about twenty-five to thirty percent came from the cimarrons, black slaves who ran from their Spanish masters. . . .

Blacks became pirates for the same reasons as other men did, but they also sought the freedom often denied them elsewhere. W. Jeffrey Bolster wrote in *Black Jacks*, "No accurate numbers of black buccaneers exist, although the impression is that they were more numerous than the proportion of black sailors in commercial or naval service at that time." It isn't known how many of the estimated 400 pirates hanged for their crimes between 1716 and 1726 were black, for the historical record fails to show this. Like their brethren who weren't given the chance to stand trial, but were sold into slavery, these pirates remain lost to history.

Cindy Vallar. "Black Pirates." Pirates and Privateers: The History of Maritime Piracy. www.cindyvallar.com/blackpirates.html.

buccaneers, they moved to the nearby island of Tortuga. The island was small—only about 20 miles long and 4 miles wide (32km by 6.4km)—but it had fresh water and good anchorage for ships. Over the years, it had been fought over by the Spanish, Dutch, French, and English, but in 1639 a French-appointed former engineer named Jean Le Vasseur became governor and took control.

Le Vasseur used his training to build a twenty-four-gun fort by the harbor, which kept the Spanish away. He also welcomed any outlaw to the island, as long as Le Vasseur was given a share of the man's plunder. By 1650 Tortuga was one of the primary pirate strongholds in the Caribbean. Konstam writes, "Tortuga lay at the north-eastern end of the Windward Passage between Cuba and Hispaniola, and this busy shipping lane became the new hunting ground for Le Vasseur's pirates."[27]

Tortuga was not the only pirate haven in the Caribbean. On the island of Jamaica, English governors Edward D'Oyley and Thomas Modyford granted letters of marque to anyone who wanted to go out and harass and plunder Spanish ships. The English privateers also attacked

French governor Jean Le Vasseur built a fort at Tortuga and turned the small port into a pirate haven.

Spanish-held towns such as Tolú in Colombia and Portobelo in Panama. Author Earle writes, "In the sixteen years following the English conquest of Jamaica in 1655, the privateers and flibustiers sacked eighteen cities, four towns and over thirty-five villages. . . . Some places were raided time and time again, . . . and smaller villages and settlements on the south coasts of Cuba and Hispaniola were ravaged even more often."[28]

Wickedest City on Earth

On Jamaica, Port Royal was the spot where pirates gathered to do business and have fun. A city of sixty-five hundred, its citizens tolerated piracy because they profited from it. The harbor held hundreds of ships, from narrow-hulled, shallow-drafted schooners to larger galleons and captured merchant ships. Warehouses held stolen merchandise. Plundered gold and silver flowed into the city. Konstam writes, "In its heyday Port Royal was larger and more prosperous than any other city in the Americas, apart from Boston."[29]

Known as the Wickedest City on Earth, the settlement also had plenty of taverns, gambling dens, and houses of prostitution. In July 1661, for instance, forty new licenses were granted for taverns in the city. One minister who arrived, planning to attend to the spiritual needs of the inhabitants, immediately left on the same ship, saying that "since the majority of its population consists of pirates, cutthroats, [prostitutes] and some of the vilest persons in the whole of the world, I felt my permanence [staying] there was of no use."[30]

Port Royal's glory was short-lived. On the morning of June 7, 1692, a massive earthquake hit the island. The tremors rocked the sandy peninsula on which the town was built, causing buildings to slide and disappear beneath the sea. An estimated two thousand Port Royalists were killed immediately in the disaster. Many more perished from injuries and disease in the following days. Some survivors, such as Anglican priest Emmanuel Heath, saw the earthquake as a sign of God's wrath and hoped that the disaster would change Port Royalists' behavior. "By this terrible Judgment," Heath stated, "God will make them reform their lives, for there was not a more ungodly People on the Face of the Earth."[31]

Brethren of the Coast

Not even an earthquake stopped the pirates of the Caribbean, who became known as the Brethren of the Coast. Based out of Port Royal and Tortuga, they attacked Spanish merchant ships, using small sailing or rowing boats called pinnaces and single-masted boats

The pirate city of Port Royal, Jamaica, was destroyed by an earthquake in 1692. Many thought it was God's wrath that led to the destruction of the wicked city.

called sloops. These light vessels allowed the pirates to hide in the shallow waters of small bays and inlets and wait for their prey, then maneuver quickly up to a larger ship and attack.

The most famous Brethren of the Coast was Henry Morgan. Morgan was born in Wales in 1635. In his teens he traveled to the Caribbean and joined a pirate crew from Tortuga. He soon was a leader of the buccaneers and friends with the Jamaican governors, from whom he received letters of marque to attack the Spanish. In 1664, with ten ships and five hundred men, he captured Puerto Principe, Cuba, then went on to take the fortified and well-protected town of Portobelo, Panama. The latter was guarded by three forts, and it is said that Morgan's men used captured Jesuit priests as human shields in taking the third. In 1669, assigned to attack the Spanish along the coast of Venezuela, Morgan took nine hundred men and nine ships and made a successful raid on the Lake Maracaibo region. He returned to Port Royal with the equivalent of about $14 million in today's money of treasure.

In January 1670 Morgan embarked on the most daring venture of his career, the capture of the city of Panama. The city was a stopover point on the over-

Henry Morgan, (center, seated) passes judgment on Portobelo citizens in 1664 after capturing the city, which was known as Spain's crown jewel in Panama.

Captured Vessels

Pirates always needed good ships in which to sail, but they did not buy and sell them like ordinary seamen would. Author David Cordingly explains in Under the Black Flag:

Unlike the Royal Navy or the East India Company or the merchants of London or Boston, the pirates could not build a ship to order. They could only acquire vessels which came their way. . . . The majority of pirate ships were prizes, ships captured by force. Operating outside the law, the pirates could not . . . go along to the prize courts to get their captured vessels valued and sold, which was the usual practice of privateer captains. Having looted a ship, the pirates would burn the vessel or set her adrift. However, if the pirate captain liked the look of the ship, he would either take her over for his own use or employ her as a consort [a member of his fleet].

David Cordingly. *Under the Black Flag: The Romance and the Reality of Life Among the Pirates.* New York: Random House, 1995, p. 160.

land route where gold and silver from the Incan Empire was transported from Peru to the Atlantic coast. Morgan's task was extremely difficult. At the time there was no Panama Canal, which greatly improved access to the city, and Morgan's band had to cross mountains and push through thick jungle to get to the city. After the difficult trek and several battles, the pirates succeeded in taking the city, which was burned in the process. Morgan and his men returned to Port Royal with treasure that included 750,000 pieces of eight (about $90 million in today's money).

The Pirate Round

The second part of the Golden Age of Piracy began in the 1690s. It was characterized by long pirate excursions that started from the Caribbean and launched out into the Atlantic and beyond to the Indian Ocean. When enough ships had been attacked and enough treasure taken, the pirates would sail back to their home port. These excursions were known as the Pirate Round, and those who made them discovered, in the words of Konstam, "[the Indian Ocean was] a pirate's dream—rich and poorly protected prizes . . . , the most lucrative pirate destination in the world."[32]

There were several reasons that some pirates went on these rounds, looking beyond the Caribbean for riches. First, by the 1690s the largest reserves of treasure had been taken from the region. Second, the devastation of Port Royal destroyed one of their chief markets for stolen goods. Third, it was from India

A Painful End

Arrogant and unrepentant, pirate William "Captain" Kidd refused to take responsibility for his actions even as he was being led to the gallows. In her article "Captain William Kidd," editor Cindy Vallar describes his execution:

Kidd's execution was set for late afternoon on Friday, 23 May [1701]. He drank a considerable amount of rum before and during the three-mile procession to Execution Dock at Wapping [England]. He slurred his words while giving his last speech in which he blamed his mutinous crew for his troubles. . . . When he finished, the hangman yanked the blocks holding up the platform, and Kidd and three others dropped. Kidd's rope broke, and he fell to the ground only to be hanged again. After the Thames River washed over his body three times, his corpse was put into an iron cage and hung from an iron gibbet [hanging cage] at Tilbury Point "as a greater Terrour to all Persons from Committing ye like Crimes for the time to come."

Quoted in Cindy Vallar. "Captain William Kidd." Pirates and Privateers: The History of Maritime Piracy. www.cindyvallar.com/williamkidd.html.

Pirate William Kidd was arrogant, unrepentant, and drunk to the end when he was hanged for piracy in 1701.

that high-value luxury goods like silk, spices, and jewels were being transported to Europe. No powerful navies operated in the waters of the Indian Ocean, so the enormous merchant ships that sailed there were open to attack and capture. The area was too tempting for adventurous men to ignore.

American Thomas Tew was the first to make the Pirate Round, setting out in his ship, the *Amity*, to the Indian Ocean and the Red Sea in 1692. His gamble paid off well. In the Red Sea in 1693, he successfully captured a warship owned by the Indian emperor Alamgir I that carried a fortune in coins, jewels, ivory, spices, and silks. When he returned to America with the treasure, he became a hero to men like Governor Benjamin Fletcher of New York, who enjoyed the friendship of pirates and accepted gifts from them. Tew was not successful for long, however. On his second voyage, in September 1695, he and his crew were pursuing a convoy of merchant ships in the Red Sea when he was hit by cannon fire and was killed. His final resting place is unknown.

Pirate Kings of Madagascar

After Tew, other pirates began making the Pirate Round. They usually set off across the Atlantic to the coast of Africa, sailed around the Cape of Good Hope, and then stopped at the island of Madagascar, where they could get fresh provisions and careen, or clean, their ship's hulls. After being at sea for months, hulls collected barnacles, weeds, and infestations of worms, which slowed ships down and damaged them.

The island was perfect for a stopover. It was close to trading routes and had plenty of coves where, at low tide, repairs could be made. The small bands of native peoples who lived there did not mind pirates coming to their shores. Antongil Bay on the northern edge of Madagascar and Nosy Boraha (St. Mary's Island), a small island off the northeast coast, were both used as bases for attacking passing merchant ships. The island was so inviting that many pirates remained there, becoming pirate "kings" rather than going back to the Caribbean. For instance, pirate Abraham Samuel set up a business as a trader on the island around 1696 and called himself the King of Port Dolphin. Another former pirate, James Plantain, was known as the King of Ranter's Bay.

Once pirates left Madagascar, the next leg of the Pirate Round was where most of the actual piracy took place. In the Persian Gulf, the Red Sea, and the Indian Ocean, the pirates attacked merchant ships, particularly the large and heavily loaded *East Indiamen*. These ships were specially designed to hold passengers and cargo and were operated under charter, or license, to any of the East India Companies of the major European trading powers. Because the *Indiamen* were fitted with cannons and had plenty of storage facilities, the pirates often kept these ships as their own for the rest of the Round. At other times, the captured ships were sailed into port and sold. No matter what the decision, once the pirates were satisfied with their loot, they turned and sailed back across the

Atlantic, sometimes stopping again in Madagascar to refit their ships or wait for favorable winds.

The Red Sea Men

Roundsmen, also known as Red Sea Men, were legendary for the riches they captured. One New Yorker wrote in the 1690s, "We have a parcel of pyrates called the Red Sea Men in these parts who got a great booty of Arabian gold."[33] Henry Every (or Avery), who captained the *Fancy*, gained renown for capturing a ship personally owned by the emperor Aurangzeb of India. The ship not only had sixty-two mounted cannons, four hundred to five hundred armed guards, and six hundred passengers, it also held treasure worth more than $100 million in today's money. In response to his attack on the ship, the East India Company offered a reward of $150,000 for Every's capture. This led to the first worldwide manhunt in history. Nevertheless, Every managed to elude his hunters. He disappeared in 1696, one of the few major pirate captains to have escaped arrest or death in battle.

Scottish pirate William "Captain" Kidd was less fortunate than Every. Kidd began his career as a privateer for the British against the French in the Caribbean, then was commissioned in 1696 by Massachusetts royal governor Richard Coote to become a pirate hunter. However, as Kidd sailed for the Indian Ocean in his ship, the *Adventure Galley*, he again had a change of heart and went back to pirating.

Kidd pirated for only two years before he met his fate. In 1698 he captured an Armenian merchant ship captained by an Englishman who escaped and sent word back to England of Kidd's crimes. A reward was put on Kidd's head, and knowing he was a wanted man, he sailed back to America and turned himself in to the governor of Boston, hoping to gain a pardon. Instead, he was arrested and sent to London. There he was put on trial and found guilty of piracy and the murder of one of his crewmen, William Moore, whom he had smashed over the head with a wooden bucket in a fit of rage in 1697. Earle writes, "He was hanged at Wapping on 23 May 1701, the victim of his own stupidity and puffed-up ambition and not one of the greatest of pirates."[34]

A Most Active Time

The third phase of the Golden Age of Piracy began sometime around 1716 and lasted until about 1726. It was characterized by a combination of piracy from the two earlier periods—plundering in the Caribbean and treasure hunting in the Indian Ocean. Shipping between Africa, the Caribbean, and Europe soared in the 1700s, providing more targets for pirates to prey upon. The end of the War of the Spanish Succession, which had involved Spain, Britain, and other European countries and had lasted from 1701 to 1714, meant that many sailors were idle and looking for work. They formed a pool of experienced men who saw piracy as a way to make a living. About two thousand pirates in some twenty-five to

A pirate vessel attacks a merchant ship in the Caribbean. Between the years 1701 and 1714, no fewer than two thousand pirates in twenty-five to thirty ships terrorized the seas—the most active period in pirate history.

thirty ships were on the seas during this most active period of pirate history.

With so many pirates on the high seas, their crimes made news both in America and Europe. Newspaper accounts warned merchants and passengers of the danger as well as provided fascinating tales of the outlaws' activities. These tales were often so dramatic that they were hard to believe. Nevertheless, they were supported by facts and provided a glimpse into the lives of the Caribbean pirates who made the Golden Age of Piracy an informative one as well.

Chapter Three

The Pirate Life

During the Golden Age of Piracy, more information became available about Caribbean pirates and their lives than ever before. Colonial governors made written reports of what they saw and heard. There were records of pirates' trials and what was said during them. Those who hunted the pirates and those who had been victimized by pirates recounted their experiences. There was also a book, *The Buccaneers of America*, published in the United States in 1684 by French author and physician Alexander Exquemelin. Exquemelin provided a firsthand account of pirates after sailing with pirate Henry Morgan and participating in some of Morgan's pirate raids.

In 1724 a book called *A General History of the Robberies and Murders of the Most Notorious Pyrates* (soon called *A General History of the Pyrates*) was published and included a great deal of factual material, some of which came from the pirates themselves. The name of the author, Captain Charles Johnson, was fictitious, but many guessed that he had been a pirate or someone like author Daniel Defoe, who had much knowledge of pirates and the sea. Cordingly writes, "Whatever the identity of the author, the book has had a far-reaching effect on popular views of pirates."[35]

Free and Equal

Details of pirates' lives revealed their desire for freedom and their disdain of rank and authority. All were rebellious of the rules and regulations of society. Many had criminal pasts, so they kept the details of their former lives hidden. As Earle writes, "Buccaneers were so determined to forget the social hierarchy of the outside world that it was forbidden to speak of a man's origins, and surnames which might have given those origins away were replaced by noms de guerre [names of war] or nicknames."[36]

Life aboard pirate ships was based on democracy at a time when few democracies existed in the world. Pirate crews had a say in the division of treasure, in compensation for the injured, and in rules of behavior. These rules were called customs of the coast, Jamaica discipline, and eventually articles of regulation.

One of the best known sets of articles was created in 1720 by pirate Bartholomew Roberts and his men. Some of their rules seem astonishing for their strictness and respectability. They set hours at which lights had to be put out—8:00 P.M. They prohibited gambling for money on board, taking women on board, and fighting on board.

Life aboard pirate ships was based on democracy. Crews had a say in determining the dividing up of treasure, the amount of compensation received for injuries, and the rules of conduct.

Marked by Battle

Because of the many hand-to-hand battles they fought, many pirates lost limbs and had ugly scars. Unlike fictional pirates, few wore eye patches, wooden legs, or other prostheses, but there were exceptions. For instance, Oruc Barbarossa, who had lost an arm in battle, was nicknamed Silver Arm for the silver prosthesis he wore. Francois Le Clerc was known as Pegleg because he had lost a leg fighting the English in 1549. Seventeenth-century Kuwaiti pirate Rahmah ibn Jabir al-Jalahimah wore an eye patch after losing an eye in battle.

Keeping Order

It was standard for most articles, including Roberts's, to state that every pirate was to have a vote on important decisions. Each was to get an equal share of any treasure that was captured, although the captain and quartermaster usually received two shares. The quartermaster ranked higher than other ships officers because he was responsible for discipline and for leading the pirate boarding party when it invaded another ship.

Pirates were not generally required to remain on a ship for any set length of time; they could come and go as they pleased. Still, they had no right to desert or disobey the captain during battle. Roberts's rules stated, "To Desert the Ship, or their Quarters in Battle, was punished with Death, or Marooning."[37] Marooning involved leaving someone on an uninhabited island to survive as best he could.

Many pirates broke the rules, but the guidelines helped keep order among those who had to live in close quarters for long periods of time. As one pirate who sailed under Captain Edward Low admitted, "If we once take the liberty of breaking our articles and oath, then there is none of us can be sure of anything."[38]

The Pirate Crew

Pirate ships were crowded places because they had so many men aboard. Merchant ships commonly had a crew of ten to eighteen, but a pirate crew could include up to three hundred. The numbers were higher for several reasons. First, there were a large number of guns that needed to be manned on pirate vessels. Also, when attacks were made, a large number of pirates were needed to swarm onto the victim ship and overcome any resistance.

The average age of a pirate was twenty-seven. Young men were more willing to put up with the discomfort of all kinds of weather that one encountered at sea.

Youthfulness was also a necessity because of the physical demands of working on a ship. This included hoisting sails and hauling on ropes as well as climbing the rigging and carrying heavy cargo.

Music helped make the hard work easier, so musicians, commonly fiddlers and accordion players, were especially valued on board a pirate ship. Musicians provided accompaniment to sea shanties, songs which pirates sang to help synchronize their movements as they performed tasks. For instance, halyard shanties were sung while the sails were raised or lowered. Windlass shanties accompanied raising the anchor. Pumping shanties attended pumping water out of the bilge, the lowest part of the ship.

From Carpenters to Gentlemen

In addition to musicians, other members of the crew were valued for their special expertise. For instance, every ship needed a doctor on board. If one did not come willingly, a doctor might be kidnapped and taken to sea against his will. Several men needed to be skilled at carpentry, both to make repairs and to do remodeling. When a merchant ship was captured and the crew members chose to take it as one of their own, carpenters were able to refit it quickly with extra guns and remove parts to make it lighter and faster.

Although some pirates had specific skills, most were poor, uneducated men. Captain Stede Bonnet was one exception. Bonnet was a gentleman, the son of a wealthy English landowner who lived on the island of Barbados. In 1717, perhaps because he was bored or unhappy with his ordinary life, he left his land and his wife behind and purchased a sloop that he named the *Revenge*. He then began attacking and plundering ships along the eastern coast of North America.

Gentleman pirate Stede Bonnet was the exception to the rule that pirates were poor and uneducated. He operated along the East Coast of America and was captured and hanged in November 1718.

Bonnet sailed with the pirate Blackbeard for a time but was pirating on his own when his ship was captured in 1718. He and his crew were tried and found guilty, and the judge emphasized Bonnet's educated background when he pronounced sentence. "Major Stede Bonnet, you stand here convict'd on 2 indictments of Pyracy. . . . You being a Gentleman that have had the advantage of a liberal education, and being generally esteemed a Man of Letters, I believe it will be needless for me to explain to you the Nature of Repentance."[39] Bonnet was hanged in November 1718 on the waterfront of Charleston, South Carolina.

Female Pirates

Another pirate who died by hanging was John "Calico Jack" Rackham, captain of the *William*. Rackham was noteworthy because two members of his crew were female. Women in piracy were rare in Europe and America. They were seen as distractions and as agents of bad luck. Rackham apparently did not worry about those potential problems. In 1719, while in the Bahamas, he met and began an affair with a woman named Anne Bonny, wife of James Bonny, a former pirate turned informant for the British government. Anne was Irish and had often passed as a boy when she was growing up, so she had no hesitation in leaving her husband, putting on men's clothes, and going off to pirate with Rackham. Johnson writes, "Anne Bonny kept him company, and when any business was to be done in their way, nobody was more forward or courageous than she."[40]

At some point when Bonny and Rackham were sailing together, another interesting newcomer joined their crew. She was an Englishwoman in disguise named Mary Read. Read had also dressed as a boy in her youth and was used to passing as a man. Both she and Bonny remained with Rackham and proved to be extremely adept at pirating, even taking part in battles with men. According to one witness, "In times of action, no Person amongst them was more resolute, or ready to Board or undertake any Thing that was hazardous."[41]

In 1720 Rackham's ship was attacked and captured by an armed sloop sent by Jamaican authorities. Rackham and his crew were taken to Jamaica, where he, Read, and Bonny were tried and sentenced to be hanged. Both women claimed to be pregnant, so they were given a stay of execution until they gave birth. Read died in April 1721 of fever probably related to childbirth, but Bonny was for some reason spared execution and managed to disappear. Before she did, however, she had last words for Rackham, who was executed on November 18, 1720. She stated she was "sorry to see him there [in prison], but if he had fought like a Man, he need not have been hang'd like a Dog."[42]

Good Luck and Bad

Like Bonny, few pirates would have sympathized with Rackham's death. They would have pointed out that he

An illustration depicts Anne Bonny, Jack Rackham, and Mary Read (left to right). Celebrated female pirates in Rackham's crew, Read died in prison and Bonny disappeared, her fate unknown. Rackham was executed.

had brought it about by taking Read and Bonny aboard his ship. Pirates took their superstitions very seriously, even though these beliefs could be contradictory. For instance, pirate superstitions held that women were bad luck on a ship, while at the same time claiming that the female form could calm a storm at sea. To satisfy such a contradictory view, pirates banned women from their ships but attached figureheads—a carved shape of a woman—to the bow as a good luck piece. These figures were colorfully painted and were usually unclothed from the waist up.

Pirates had other superstitions, besides those relating to women. For instance, they preferred not to set sail on Fridays because this was the day that Jesus was crucified, and they believed the voyage would be unsuccessful. Sailing on Friday the thirteenth was doubly unlucky. On the other hand, the seventeenth and the twenty-ninth of any month were considered good days to set sail, particularly if the voyage was going to last many months.

Sharks following in the wake of a ship were thought to be unlucky and meant someone aboard would soon die. Manta rays, also known as devilfish or sea devils, were feared as much as sharks because they were believed to attach themselves to a ship's anchor and drag the ship under the water. Small seabirds known as stormy petrels were good luck because they were supposedly sent from Mary, the mother of Jesus, to warn pirates of coming storms. Tattoos and piercings were good luck as well and may have explained why many pirates were tattooed and wore gold hoop earrings.

Ragtag and Colorful

In the days when men traditionally wore somber clothing, including long-tailed coats and top hats, pirates were known for their casual, ragtag appearance, including their multicolor mix of

Pirates were known for their casual, ragtag appearance, which sometimes included multicolored clothing and outlandish tattoos.

clothing. Some who were ex-seamen started out in outfits called slops, which consisted of canvas jackets, with or without sleeves, and breeches that reached the knees. They also wore knitted caps called Monmouth caps, stockings, linen shirts, and shoes. This outfit changed as pieces wore out and as pirates picked up replacement apparel. The replacements could include anything from bandanas and three-cornered hats to buckled shoes and coats with large, gold buttons.

Pirates accessorized themselves with an assortment of weapons, especially when an attack was to be made. For instance, Blackbeard went into battle with a short sword called a cutlass, three pairs of pistols strapped across his chest, and daggers and pistols in his belt. Although guns at the time were not as accurate as the guns of today, pirates practiced extensively and were often very accurate. According to historian Earle, "The buccaneers were able to hit a coin spinning at 120 paces or to sever an orange from a tree by its stalk. . . . They were certainly effective marksmen."[43]

Some pirates added to their colorful appearance by carrying parrots or even monkeys perched on their shoulders. Parrots were picked up in exotic ports in South America and Africa and were particularly popular because they could be taught to talk and could be presented to officials as gifts or bribes. Pirate William Dampier wrote of the parrots he and his crewmates collected in the West Indies: "There was scarce a man but what sent aboard one or two of them. So that with provision, chests, hen-coops and parrot-cages, our ships were full."[44]

Jolly Rogers

When getting ready to attack their victims, pirates hoisted flags on their ships that were distinctive, identifiable, and known as Jolly Rogers. The name came from the fact that the pirate flags were at first solid red and called *jolie rouge*, or "pretty red," by the French.

Pirates soon flew black as well as red flags and added designs on them. A black flag indicated that victims could surrender and not be killed, whereas a red one meant that the pirates were going to fight to the death and show no mercy. Captain Richard Hawkins, who was captured by pirates in 1724, reports that "when they fight under Jolly Roger, they give quarter [clemency], which they do not when they fight under the red or bloody flag."[45]

Although in fiction Jolly Roger flags often carried a skull and crossbones, real flags were distinct to their owner. Blackbeard's flag portrayed a devilish skeleton spearing a red heart. Bartholomew Roberts had two flags. One showed a figure of himself and a skeleton holding an hourglass, and the other showed a figure of himself standing on two skulls. Calico Jack Rackham's flag had a skull and crossed swords.

Pirate Atrocities

As their flags portrayed, real pirates were often cruel cutthroats who tortured, raped, and killed their victims. By modern standards, some would be

The Elegant Pirate

When it came to appearance, Bartholomew Roberts, who sailed the seas between 1719 and 1722, was considered one of the most elegantly dressed pirates of the Golden Age. Described as a tall, handsome man, he loved expensive clothes and jewelry. During one battle he wore a crimson vest, a scarlet plumed hat, and on his chest, a massive gold chain with a diamond cross hanging from it.

As unusual as his clothing, Roberts drank tea, forbade gambling, and encouraged prayer on his ship. Still, he was one of the most successful pirates of the Golden Age. He led a fleet of pirate ships that was so menacing that naval ships turned back at the sight of it. He was believed to have captured almost five hundred ships during his pirate career.

As with most pirates, Roberts's luck ran out before he grew old. In February 1722 the British government sent a warship and a party of men to find and capture him. During their attack on his ship, the *Royal Fortune*, he was killed. Without their captain, the crew lost its nerve and surrendered, but not before they weighted Roberts's body down and buried it at sea, where it was never found.

Pirate Bartholomew Roberts was known for his elegant attire. He captured about five hundred ships during his career.

considered psychopaths—persons who commit antisocial and violent acts and feel no sorrow or guilt for what they have done.

Dutch pirate Roche Brasiliano was one of these most brutal men. He operated in the Caribbean in the 1660s, and according to author Exquemelin, "He perpetrated the greatest atrocities possible against [his enemies] the Spaniards. Some of them he tied or spitted on wooden stakes and roasted them alive between two fires, like killing a pig."[46] Even while ashore, Brasiliano would run up and down streets, attacking, beating, and wounding anyone who crossed his path.

Edward Low, who sailed from 1690 to 1724, also had a violent temper and killed without provocation. For instance, when he became annoyed at the quality of the meals prepared by a captured French ship's cook, he decided that the man was "a greasy fellow, [who] would fry well in the fire"[47] The cook was tied to the main mast and burnt with his ship. When another ship's captain offended Low, he cut off the victim's ears, slit his nose, and hacked up his body. Despite his horrible reputation, Low was never captured and was last heard of sailing near Africa. Johnson observes, "I have heard that he talked of going to Brazil . . . , though the best information we could receive, would be, that he and all his crew were at the bottom of the sea."[48]

Terror at Sea

Not all pirates were as cruel as Brasiliano and Low, but torture was regularly used to find out where treasure was hidden, when other ships were sailing, and other valuable information. Common tortures included beating victims, hanging them by their wrists or genitals, "woolding" them by tightening knotted cords around their head, or placing them in a barrel of gunpowder and threatening them with incineration.

Walking the plank was a torture often referred to in fiction, but it was practiced only rarely in actuality. In 1822, for instance, William Smith, captain of the British sloop *Blessing*, was forced to walk the plank by the Spanish pirate crew in the West Indies. In two cases in 1829, crews of the packet *Redpole* and the Dutch brig *Vhan Fredericka* were murdered by walking the plank.

Walking the plank was especially fearsome because the victim usually had his hands bound and had a heavy weight tied around the neck. The terror of the experience was heightened when the waters around the ship were infested by sharks.

"Fierce and Wild"

There is no record that Edward Teach, or Blackbeard, ever made anyone walk the plank. Teach was born in England and began pirating in the Caribbean in 1717. On his ship *Queen Anne's Revenge*, a former cargo vessel, he led a group of pirates based out of New Providence, an island in the Bahamas.

New Providence was a pirate stronghold between 1715 and 1725, the late part of the Golden Age of Piracy. Like Port Royal, the harbor at the town of

Blackbeard had a ferocious reputation, but he never tortured his captives. His personal appearance was said to be frightening.

Nassau, New Providence, easily accommodated hundreds of pirate ships but was too shallow for the larger Royal Navy vessels to enter. British governor Woodes Rogers helped bring law and order to the Bahamas in 1718, but by then Blackbeard had moved on and was plundering along the Carolinas.

Although he had a ferocious reputation, Blackbeard never tortured those he held in captivity. He commanded his ships with the permission of his crews and relied on his fierce looks to terrify his victims and get their cooperation. A tall man, he grew his black hair and beard extremely long and twisted it into ribbons and tails. When going into battle he stuck lighted matches into his beard on each side of his face so his head was wreathed in smoke. Johnson writes, "His Eyes, naturally looking Fierce and Wild, made him altogether such a Figure, that Imagination cannot form an idea of a Fury, from hell, to look more frightful."[49]

Drinking and Carousing

Whether pirates captured a ship by force or by cleverness, they often destroyed much of the treasure in the riotous celebration that followed. Silk fabric was trampled, works of art were broken, and alcohol was consumed. Many cargoes included rum, which was made in the Caribbean in the 1600s and was regularly shipped to Europe to supply drinking needs there.

In addition to rum, pirate ships had on board a kind of alcoholic drink known as grog or bumboo. Bumboo was a mixture of rum, water, sugar, and nutmeg. It was not as strong as straight rum, so pirates could drink it in moderate quantities and still be ready to work when necessary.

Pirates also celebrated by eating any delicacies that were found on board the captured ships. Ordinary pirate food included hardtack biscuits (similar to crackers), salmagundi—a stew of whatever the cook had on hand, which could include chopped meat, fish, onions, eggs, and spices—salted beef, eggs if there were chickens on board, and pickled vegetables. Therefore, any change of menu was welcome, and after capturing a ship, pirates ate and enjoyed themselves without a thought for good manners or saving anything for another day. George Francis Dow and John Henry Edmonds write, "They passed the time away, drinking and carousing merrily, before and after dinner, which they eat in a very disorderly manner, more like a

Good Eats

After a long period at sea eating hard biscuits and dried meat, pirates were ready to try other delicacies when they came ashore. In Under the Black Flag, *David Cordingly describes some of what they ate:*

During . . . trips ashore the men would catch turtles, which could be found in great numbers among the West Indian islands: "the choice of all for fine eating is the turtle or sea tortoise," wrote Francis Rogers when he visited Jamaica in 1704. "The flesh looks and eats much like choice veal, but the fat is of a green color, very luscious and sweet; the liver is likewise green, very wholesome. . . ." The pirates would shoot birds for the cooking pot and hunt cattle, goats, or pigs if they could be found. Sometimes they had to resort to more unusual provisions. On the coast of South America the buccaneers led by Captain [Bartholomew] Sharp were eating ". . . monkeys, snakes, oysters, conchs, periwinkles . . . with some other sorts of good fish."

David Cordingly. *Under the Black Flag: The Romance and the Reality of Life Among the Pirates.* New York: Random House, 1995, p. 95.

kennel of hounds, than like men, snatching and catching the victuals [food] from one another."[50]

Pieces of Eight

More important than food or drink was the treasure that remained. As in fiction, ships often carried chests of coins. Some of the most well-known were Spanish silver dollars, also called pieces of eight because they were the equivalent of eight reals (another Spanish silver coin). Other coins that made up pirate treasure were gold doubloons, equal to 32 reals.

Legend has it that pirates commonly buried chests of coins and treasure and then created maps so they or other pirates could relocate them. No authentic treasure maps have ever been found, however, probably because most pirates quickly spent their treasure or fenced it (sold it to a trader). There were a few exceptions. Privateer Sir Francis Drake buried Spanish gold and silver that he captured in Panama while returning to his ships. He returned a short time later, however, dug up the loot, and took it back to England. Pirate William Kidd allegedly buried some of his wealth on Long Island when he feared he was going to be caught. He hoped to use its location as a bargaining tool with the authorities, but he failed. Only part of that treasure was found. Under pain of torture, Roche Brasiliano confessed to burying treasure on Isla de Pinos (now Isla de la Juventud) near Cuba. When soldiers went to the island, they found in excess of one thousand pieces of eight.

Despite the lure of treasure, by the 1730s the chances of pirates being able to steal a fortune were slim. Their attacks had affected too many countries, and tolerance for them was wearing thin. European nations were building up their navies in order to offer greater protection for merchants and to hunt down the outlaws. Earle writes, "And so at last the golden age of piracy came to an end. The freedom- and drink-loving pirates had their moment of fame, but in the long run the navy, the law and the self-destructive nature of the pirates themselves ensured that piracy was not an occupation with a very long life expectancy."[51]

Such was not the case in Asia, however. Though less famous than their European counterparts, Asian pirates pillaged ships and villages long after the Golden Age of Piracy faded. Under their influence, piracy flourished in the South China Sea and pirate empires were built that lasted hundreds of years.

Chapter Four

Piracy in Asia

While pirates were raiding the Mediterranean and the Caribbean and making the Pirate Round, piracy was occurring in Asia as well. From India to Malaysia, generations of men and women stole from merchant vessels that sailed the eastern seas. Konstam writes, "In Chinese waters the threat of piracy remained constant for seafarers for more than a thousand years, probably longer. The first recorded incident . . . in the South China Sea took place in A.D. 589. . . . However, it is almost a certainty that piracy flourished long before."[52]

Junks on the South China Sea

The South China Sea is the part of the Pacific Ocean that lies south of mainland China, west of the Philippines, and north of Indonesia. As in other parts of the world, piracy existed there because people living along the coasts were skilled at navigation and were desperate enough to steal to make a living. Like the Barbary and Caribbean pirates, no governments or navies could stop them, because these men were familiar with the area and could hide from their pursuers. Even when the powerful Ming dynasty arose in China, it was unable to abolish the practice. In fact, money spent by governments to suppress piracy was often channeled through corrupt officials to pirates who used it to increase their own power.

In making their attacks, Asian pirates relied on a traditional boat called the junk. The name comes from the Malay word *dgong*, or *jong*. The junk was a wide, flat-bottomed vessel, invented as early as the second century B.C. It was commonly used as a merchant or warship. Junks had up to four masts with triangular bamboo sails, and their holds were divided into small compartments so that the entire ship would not flood if one part was damaged. Some of the largest junks measured over 100 feet (30.5m) and had more than two hundred persons in a crew. The average, however, was around 45 feet (14m) with just a few dozen crew members.

Pirates converted merchant junks to pirate ships by adding ten to thirty large guns, including at least one *lantaka*, or swivel gun, which they could use to clear enemy decks of any opposition. Between attacks, crews usually slept on deck or in the hold. Historian H. Warington Smyth states, "As an engine for carrying man and his commerce upon the high and stormy seas as well as on the vast inland waterways, it is doubtful if any class of vessel . . . is more suited or better adapted to its purpose than the Chinese or Indian junk."[53]

Bugis and Wokou

Sailing in their junks, some of the earliest Asian pirates were Indonesian and Malaysian. As early as the 1400s, for instance, the Orang Laut pirates of Malaysia attacked ships in the Strait of Malacca, while pirates from Borneo (governed by the countries of Brunei, Indonesia, and Malaysia) struck ships

Shown here is a model of an ancient Chinese junk. Some of the largest junks were over one hundred feet long and had crews of around two hundred.

Feared for their ruthlesness, the Buginese pirates targeted Dutch and British East Indies trading ships in the seventeenth and eighteenth centuries.

in the waters between Singapore and Hong Kong. The Buginese pirates, or Bugis, of Indonesia targeted Dutch and British East Indies trading ships in the 1600s and 1700s and were known for their ruthlessness and for taking their victims unawares. Camouflaging their ships and themselves in black, they attacked merchant ships in the dark of night, creating great fear. Some believe that when word of them made its way back to Europe, their actions formed the basis for boogeyman stories that frightened children for generations.

The Wokou were other well-known pirates that sailed out of Japan beginning in the twelfth century. Early Wokou came from the ranks of Japanese farmers and fishermen, but in later centuries Chinese, Korean, and other ethnicities joined them as well. No one knows their exact numbers, but at times they ran as few as twenty junks and at other times up to four hundred. Not only did they attack ships and steal the goods on board, but they also plundered coastlines and extorted tribute from Chinese leaders eager to keep them away from their cities.

One of the worst periods of Wokou piracy was the decade between 1376 and 1385, when 174 instances of pirate raids were recorded against Korea alone. Some of these raids involved bands of as many as three thousand pirates, who looted grain and took captives to be used as slaves or to be held for ransom. Another active Wokou period was in the 1500s. Between 1523 and 1588 the Wokou made sixty-six raids on Zhejiang Province on the coast of China, an average of one attack a year. During this period pirate chief Wang Zhi was one of the best known of the Wokou. Wang headed a large, well-armed fleet that attacked official establishments such as county and district treasuries, as well as pillaging the countryside at large. Because of him and other Wokou, townspeople and villagers along the coast built tall fences around their settlements for added security.

The Great Warrior

By the mid-sixteenth century, the Wokou had almost entirely disappeared. This was due in part to new trade policies between China and other countries. Because of these policies, more European and American ships came to the East, and the naval power that arrived to protect those ships was an added force in fighting and capturing pirates.

Pirate activity soon arose in other parts of Asia, however. Notable action took place off the west coast of India, where privateer and warrior Kanhoji Angre led a fleet of ships during the eighteenth century. He and his men operated out of great rowing vessels called *ghurabs*, nicknamed grabs by the Europeans. These had up to three sails and could carry numerous cannons. According to some, when the sails were spread, the *ghurabs* looked like massive cities at sea. The pirates also used smaller galivats, which had only two masts and were more easily navigated close to the coastline.

Colorful, but fierce, East Indies pirates led by Kanhoji Angre terrorized the shipping lanes of the Indian Ocean in the eighteenth century.

Angre was a member of the Maratha (warrior) class in India and was the first notable chief of the Maratha navy. In 1698 he was also given control of the western coast of India from Bombay (now Mumbai) to Vingoria (now Vengurla). That stretch of land included twenty-six forts that had been built for defense purposes. Angre made one of them—Vijaydurg—his primary stronghold. The literal meaning of *Vijaydurg* is "Victory Fort," and it was located on a small island close to shore. It had been built about A.D. 1200 and included several unique architectural features. There was a shipbuilding facility, an undersea wall that was invisible to attacking ships, and a triple ring of fortifications. An undersea and underground tunnel also ran from the fort to an estate in the nearby village of Girye.

National Hero

Angre spent most of his privateer career making bold attacks against large British, Dutch, and Portuguese trading ships that carried goods from India to the West. Those ships belonged to countries that had colonized India, and many Indians resented the occupation of their country by outsiders. Because of

his reputation for success against such strong opponents, men from all over the world were willing to crew for Angre. These included Indian sailors as well as European mercenaries who were loyal to whomever paid them well. Angre's own ship was manned by a crew of Dutch sailors, and his chief gunner was a former Jamaican pirate.

With men, ships, and strongholds, Angre built a reputation for being invincible. He extorted tribute from Indian and British shipping companies. In 1712 he seized the armed yacht of the East India Company's governor and held it for a sizable ransom. In 1721 he repelled a British attack on Fort Vijaydurg using specially built gunships. By 1722 Angre's repeated success against the British East India Company led it to abandon any attempts to defeat him.

Angre died on June 4, 1729, never having been defeated in battle. It was said by an unidentified source that "had he been in England, like Drake, he would have been knighted and lionised as a national hero, but in India he died merely as an independent ruler who never permitted any foreign ruler to filch [take] even a part of his precious little dominion."[54] Recognition finally came in 1951, when the Western Naval Command of the Indian Navy was named INS (Indian Naval Ship) *Angre* in his honor. A statue of Angre also stands in the Naval Dockyard in Mumbai.

Chinese Pirate Empires

While pirates like Angre sailed the seas for relatively short spans of time, Chinese pirates were a long-term problem for Asia. Due to weak governments and the support of regional warlords who dominated sections of the coastline, some pirates were able to form powerful empires that allowed them to pillage and plunder with little fear of consequences. Their attacks were sometimes aimed at those they disagreed with politically, but unlike European and Barbary privateers, few Chinese pirates had the backing of a government sponsor while they were sailing the seas.

The first of the three most powerful Chinese pirate empires arose in the 1600s. It was headed by a former businessman named Zheng Zhilong from the Fujian Province opposite the island of Taiwan. Zheng and his fleet of over eight hundred junks sailed up and down the coast, attacking shipping in the mouth of the Yangtze River and as far south as Vietnam. They also demanded and received protection money from shipowners in order to allow them to stay in business.

Zheng caused so much disruption that the head of the Ming dynasty named him admiral of coastal waters and gave him control of the province of Fukien in the hopes that he would give up his lawless ways. Zheng ruled under the Ming dynasty until 1649. At that time he changed loyalties and allowed a competing dynasty, the Manchus, to capture the province. He continued to rule under the Manchus until the anti-Manchu activities of his son, Zheng Chenggong, became too much for authorities to overlook. Held accountable for his son's activities, Zheng was executed in 1661.

Female Pirates

Female pirates were more powerful in Asia than in other parts of the world, but many women went into piracy for the same reasons no matter where they originated. Author Cathy Converse explains in "The Lady Was a Pirate."

There are various reasons why women chose to become pirates. Many women were connected with male pirate leaders, working on their father's, husband's or lover's ship or were pushed into it by unscrupulous men. In most cases piracy seemed the best available option for them. Usually women pirates came from poverty stricken circumstances where prostitution or low-waged personal service was a more common route for industrious women to survive. Given access to ships and the sea, contacts and opportunity, some women chose a life of piracy instead. And why not, they reasoned, for with few exceptions each pirate received an equal share of the spoils, the food was better and life in general was more comfortable. They became self-sufficient and depended on no man nor fickle social circumstance for survival. The life of a pirate offered women extraordinary mobility, with the chance of doing well financially—for Cheng I Sao [Zheng Yi Sao, or Madam Zheng] it was total control over the China merchant trade.

Cathy Converse. "The Lady Was a Pirate." The Nautical Institute. www.nauticalinstitute.ca/Articles/files/lady_pirate.htm.

Madam Zheng (right) was one of many female Chinese pirates who menaced shipping vessels in the eighteenth century.

Defender and Outlaw

The second pirate empire began immediately after Zheng Zhilong's death, when Zheng Chenggong, or Koxinga, assumed his father's position as a pirate leader. A strong supporter of the Ming dynasty, Koxinga concentrated his attacks on Manchu ships, which he plundered and sank. He also used his pirate fleet to lead raids against Manchu-held cities, becoming so successful that the emperor had to order the inhabitants of eighty sea towns to move inland to avoid his attacks.

Koxinga's pirate empire survived into the 1680s despite heavy losses sustained in a failed attempt to drive the Manchu forces from Nanking in 1659. He maintained a tight hold on regional trade for almost twenty-five years, took on Dutch traders who operated in his region, and captured the island of Formosa (now Taiwan) from the Dutch in 1662.

Despite his ability to wield power, Koxinga did not live to an old age. In 1683 he died of malaria at the age of fifty-nine. Although he had been an outlaw all his life, he is remembered in China as a hero. Konstam writes, "Today, . . . (Koxinga) is seen as a hero, both in Taiwan and in mainland China, where his reputation as a defender of Ming culture and civilization seems to have outweighed his crimes as a pirate warlord."[55]

Zheng Yi

The third Chinese pirate empire was the most powerful of the three. Famine in 1799 drove many Chinese farmers to become pirates, with entire families of men, women, and children roaming the seas looking for merchant ships to attack. A man named Zheng Yi took advantage of this source of manpower when he began building a coalition of small pirate fleets beginning in 1801.

Zheng Yi was the son of a pirate and was experienced in the trade. In 1801 he married a former prostitute named Ching Shih, and together they put together an alliance of pirates that regularly attacked ships around the Canton area. By 1805 Zheng Yi commanded so many ships that he divided them into six fleets, each known by a color—black, red, white, blue, yellow, and green. Each fleet was assigned an area in which to operate. Zheng Yi remained with the Red Fleet but retained control over the others to insure that they did not fight or interfere with each other's operations. The fleets also stood by to help each other if necessary. Konstam writes, "If one pirate fleet was threatened, the other colored fleets would be summoned, and the threat would be repelled."[56]

By the time Zheng Yi died in 1807, his empire numbered as many as twelve hundred junks and 150,000 pirates. His Red Fleet alone numbered six hundred junks crewed by thirty thousand men. Konstam writes, "Protection money was demanded from Chinese merchants and coastal communities, and [Zheng Yi's] junks seemed able to roam at will, attacking ships or demanding payment with impunity [without fear of punishment]."[57] Zheng Yi was still at the height of his power when he was

The Adopted Son

Cheung Pao Tsai, the adopted son of pirates Zheng Yi and Ching Shih, was a powerful pirate in his own right. Born in 1783, the son of a fisherman in southern China, he was kidnapped when he was fifteen. He later took over his adoptive parents' business, married his adopted father's widow, and led a group of fifty thousand pirates and six hundred ships as they harassed the Guangdong coastal area during the Qing dynasty. His men were well disciplined, shared captured treasure equally, and were not allowed to injure or kill women. In 1810 he gave up piracy, however, joined the Royal Navy, and ended his life in a comfortable government position.

Cheung was believed to have hidden some of his pirate treasure during his lifetime, and there are many rumors of where it might be hidden. The most popular spot is a small cave on Cheung Chau island, 6.2 miles (10km) southwest of Hong Kong. The cave has been named after Cheung. It is small and difficult to crawl into, but many tourists visit the island attraction every year.

washed overboard during a storm at sea and died.

Madam Zheng

When Zheng Yi died, his wife, who was known as Zheng Yi Sao (Zheng Yi's wife) or Madam Zheng, inherited his pirate empire and proved to be as formidable a leader as her husband. Madam Zheng had a reputation for fierceness and skill, but she recognized that she needed support as well. She appointed her husband's adopted son, Cheung Pao Tsai, as leader of the Red Fleet.

Soon after, the two started a romantic relationship, were later married, and had a son. Together they expanded the Red Fleet to two thousand junks and more than seventy thousand men. In addition to demanding protection money and attacking ships and communities, they even attacked the Chinese emperor's warships in 1808.

The attack led the emperor to declare war against Madam Zheng's pirate confederation, while also offering a pardon to any of her pirates who wanted to turn themselves in. It was the right time for Madam Zheng to end her career at sea. Her colored fleets had begun to fight among each other, and some members had decided to become pirate hunters. In 1810, as her empire split apart, she and Cheung took the government's pardon. Cheung was allowed to join the army, where he received the rank of lieutenant and command of a private fleet of twenty junks. He died in 1822 at age thirty-six. Not content with a lawful life, Madam Zheng took on the businesses of gambling and smuggling. Before her death in 1844, she allegedly ran the biggest opium-smuggling operation on the Chinese coast.

Continued Activity

Piracy continued in Asia through the 1800s, although the ethnicity of the

Chinese pirates attack a European ship off Shanghai in 1923. Between World War I and World War II, fifty-one such attacks were recorded off the China coast.

Pirate Queen

Author and explorer Aleko E. Lilius became famous for his 1930 book I Sailed with Chinese Pirates, *in which he recounts his adventures in the South China Sea. One of those adventures involved meeting pirate queen Lai Choi San and her crew, whom he calls "the most merciless gang of high-seas robbers in the world." Lilius writes:*

What a woman she was! Rather slender and short, her hair jet black, with jade pins gleaming in the knot at the neck, her ear-rings and bracelets of the same precious apple-green stone. She was exquisitely dressed in a white satin robe fastened with green jade buttons, and green silk slippers. She wore a few plain gold rings on her left hand; her right hand was unadorned. Her face and dark eyes were intelligent . . . purely Mongolian, of course—and rather hard. She was probably not yet forty.

Every move she made and every word she spoke told plainly that she expected to be obeyed, and as I had occasion to learn later, she *was* obeyed.

Aleko E. Lilius. *I Sailed with Chinese Pirates.* All Things Ransome. www.allthingsransome.net/literary/toplil.htm.

pirates changed. In the 1830s, 1840s, and 1850s, Asian pirates were joined by British, American, and French renegades who prowled the South China Sea. The latter three came to the region as a result of foreign trade. American pirate Eli Boggs was an example of one of the outsiders who had a fleet of thirty or more junks and conducted raids on English clipper ships. Boggs was known for being handsome and charming, as *London Times* correspondent George Wingrove Cook testified in 1857: "It was a face of feminine beauty. . . . Large lustrous eyes; a mouth the smile of which might woo a coy maiden; affluent black hair, not carelessly parted, . . . such was the Hong Kong pirate Eli Boggs."[58] Although handsome, Boggs was also cruel. In one case he had the body of a captured Chinese merchant cut into small pieces and delivered to shore in small buckets as a warning against interference in his criminal activities.

The twentieth century saw continued pirate activity in Asia. Between 1921 and 1929 there were twenty-nine major pirate attacks on river steamers, cargo ships, and other vessels off the coast of southern China. Fifty-one major attacks were recorded off the Asian coast between World War I and World War II. In December 1947 the Dutch ship *Van Heutz* was captured by Asian pirates who robbed the passengers of more than ninety thousand dollars.

Even up to the present day, the oceans around Asia have been the site of piracy, hijacking, and murder. But the problem is not confined to Asia; other parts of the world are plagued by modern piracy, too. And, whether in the South China Sea or off the coast of Somalia, authorities have found that today's pirates are just as ruthless as their predecessors and just as hard to control. Maritime expert Nur Jale wrote in 2009, "After a long absence, the world's seas have once again become the pirate's playground. Piracy is on the rise, . . . and is becoming increasingly complex, better organized, and more violent."[59]

Chapter Five

Piracy in Modern Times

In the twenty-first century, 90 percent of the world's trade is moved by ship. And just like in the past, desperate and lawless individuals have discovered that there is a fortune to be made by stealing those ships and the cargo that travels by sea. As a result, maritime piracy remains a significant issue in the modern world. At least 306 attacks occurred worldwide in 2008; 406 in 2009; and 445 in 2010. An estimated $13 billion to $16 billion is lost to piracy per year. Attacks take place from Colombia in South America to the Caspian Sea between Europe and Asia. As of 2011, however, the Strait of Malacca and the waters between the Red Sea and the Indian Ocean off the Somali coast have seen the most problems and have been the hardest hit.

Strait of Malacca

The Strait of Malacca is a 550-mile stretch (805km) of water between the Malaysian Peninsula and the Indonesian island of Sumatra. It is extremely narrow, only 1.7 miles (2.7km) across at one point. In the 1800s the strait was an important passageway for commercial ships traveling between China and India. In modern times it is part of the route between the busy ports of eastern Asia and ports in Europe and the Middle East. Over sixty thousand ships pass through the strait annually. They carry one-quarter of the world's traded goods, including oil, Indonesian coffee, and manufactured articles from China.

The strait is a challenge for shipowners and mariners because their ships must slow down to navigate its length. Once slowed down, the ships are easy for pirates to attack. The strait is also dotted with thousands of small islands, ideal locations for pirates to hide and avoid capture. In the year 2000 there were 75 pirate attacks in the Strait of Malacca, 28 in 2003, 38 in 2004, and 79

A Malaysian police boat intercepts a pirate vessel in the Strait of Malacca in 2007. The strait is dotted with thousands of islands, making it an ideal area for piracy.

in 2005. So great was the continuing risk that in 2005 the renowned insurance company Lloyds of London began charging more to insure anything that would pass through the area.

In addition to the physical aspects of the strait that encourage piracy, pirates have taken advantage of the fact that the waterway is not under the control of a single country. Indonesia controls the majority of the sea-lane, but Malaysia and Singapore, an independent city-state, control the rest. All of these areas have different maritime security policies. Different agencies are responsible for different aspects of piracy in Malaysia, making for bureaucratic complications and slowdowns. Indonesia and other cash-strapped governments have not been able to afford adequate coast guard and naval forces, so patrol of their territories is incomplete. These inconsistencies mean that pirates can move from one country's jurisdiction to another and evade pursuit and capture.

The Lanuns

The majority of modern pirates who prowl the waters around Asia are of Indonesian origin and are called Lanuns (Malay for *pirates*). Most are native seafaring people who live in coastal villages along the strait. Most are poor, and some are outlaws who have turned to piracy as a means of easy profit. They steal cash and electronics that can be found on board ships that they hijack. Some earn wages by working for corrupt customs or coast guard officials who profit from piracy. Others are part of organized crime syndicates. They not only rob crews, they kidnap seamen for ransom and sometimes steal entire ships, a practice known as ship-jacking. The pirates quickly paint the ship another color, change its name, and create forged identity papers. They are then able to sell it to a purchaser who has been lined up in advance.

Rather than carrying out their attacks in junks or sailing ships, as pirates in the past have done, the Lanuns rely on small motorboats, called pancungs, whose engines have been modified for optimum speed. Carrying assault rifles, pistols, and knives known as parangs—heavy-bladed machetes with razor sharp blades—they approach quickly and make the leap from their own boats to the larger vessel using ropes or bamboo poles. Once on board, they hijack the crew members, set them adrift in small boats, or kill them. Like their predecessors, modern pirates are merciless and predatory. Captain Pottengal Mukundan, director of the International Maritime Bureau (IMB), adds, "There's nothing romantic about piracy. These are ruthless people who are heavily armed and prey on people that are weaker than them."[60]

Lost at Sea

Because many Lanun attacks occur at sea, some instances of piracy go unreported. Crews disappear and only the remains of a ship are found. Authorities are left guessing about what actually happened.

What Is Piracy?

The following acts are included in the modern definition of piracy:

- boarding
- extortion
- hostage taking
- kidnapping of people for ransom
- murder
- robbery
- sabotage resulting in the ship subsequently sinking
- seizure of items or the ship
- shipwrecking

Such was the case of the *Nagasaki Spirit*, an oil tanker that was passing through the Strait of Malacca in 1992 when it collided with a container vessel, the *Ocean Blessing*. A massive fire immediately broke out and gutted both ships. All but two crew members of the *Ocean Blessing* were discovered dead onboard, but the crew of the *Nagasaki Spirit* was not found.

Authorities speculate that pirates had boarded one or both ships, overpowered the crews, and then had been unable to keep the vessels from colliding. Rear Admiral P.P. Sivamani of the Indian Navy observed, "The example of the *Ocean Blessing* . . . poses more questions than elicits answers."[61]

Despite the risk of losing their ships, their merchandise, and their crews, commercial shipping companies continue to send their ships through the strait rather than take a longer route. The time and cost are too great otherwise, as journalist Eric Koo emphasizes; "Running long, round-about sea voyages to avoid pirates is simply not cost-effective."[62]

Trouble in Somalia

While the Strait of Malacca has been one of the most pirate-plagued regions of the modern world, piracy off the Somali coast is quickly overshadowing it. Somalia is a country on the northeast coast of Africa. It is bordered by Kenya to the south, the Gulf of Aden to the north, the Indian Ocean to the east, and Ethiopia to the west. The region is part of the Horn of Africa, a 772,200-square-mile peninsula (2 million sq. km) that juts out into the Arabian Sea.

Naval vessels from Indonesia, Singapore, and Malaysia participate in a joint exercise to patrol for pirates in the Strait of Malacca.

British naval forces intercept and board two Somalian pirate vessels in the Gulf of Aden, off the coast of Somalia. There are four main groups of pirates operating from Somalia.

From 1991 to the present, Somalia has endured civil war and the lack of a strong central government. The country's provisional government does not control the semi-independent regional governments of Somaliland and Puntland, both in northeastern Somalia. Security forces are weak, and corruption is widespread. Tribal or clan struggles add to the disruption, so criminal networks are able to operate freely.

Foreign companies who took advantage of the disruption in Somalia in the 1990s also created justification for piracy in the minds of some Somalians. The native fishing industry was hard-hit after commercial fishing companies from Europe, Arabia, and Asia began illegally fishing off the Somali coast and illegally dumping industrial waste in offshore areas. With no effective coast guard to protect their shores, locals felt justified attacking the intruders. Maritime risks consultant Michael G. Frodl writes, "When [fighting off foreign fishermen] proved ineffective, some realized that 'fishing' for foreign ships [piracy] was more rewarding than going after dwindling fish stocks."[63]

Armed and Organized

In recent years at least four pirate groups have been identified in Somalia. The Puntland Group is composed of former

Journey of Terror

British journalist Colin Freeman and photographer Jose Cendon were captured by Somali pirates in November 2008 and released in January 2009. In an article titled "Paul and Rachel Chandler: Free at Last," Freeman describes his period of captivity:

Like British yachters Paul and Rachel Chandler, who were released from captivity yesterday [November 14, 2010], I too have sampled the buccaneers' spartan hospitality, after being kidnapped while reporting on their activities back in late 2008. My photographer and I were held in a series of caves, living on goat meat, rice and Rothmans [cigarettes], and fearing, like the Chandlers, that we'd end up losing either our lives, our health or our sanity. . . .

As it turned out, we were reasonably well-treated—save for one day when one of the kidnappers threatened to beat me senseless with the butt of his gun. By hostage standards, that counts as small beer, but believe me, just the threat is enough. For the rest of my time in captivity, I feared I'd end up getting tortured, in addition to my raft of existing worries about falling ill, being sold on to Islamists, or simply kept for years and years. A bit pessimistic, I grant you, but spending all day in the company of armed outlaws tends to have that effect.

Colin Freeman. "Paul and Rachel Chandler: Free at Last." Telegraph, November 15, 2010. www.telegraph.co.uk/news/worldnews/africaandindianocean/somalia/8133448/Paul-and-Rachel-Chandler-Free-at-last.html.

Upon their release in January 2009, journalist Colin Freeman (right) and photographer José Cendon discuss the three months they were held captive by Somali pirates.

fishermen from the Puntland region. The Marka, or Merca, group is based around the town of Merca. The National Volunteer Coast Guard is made up of former fishermen who at first tried to guard the coast and now specialize in intercepting small boats and fishing vessels off the southern coast of Somalia.

The fourth group is the most powerful and sophisticated and is known as the Somali Marines. It has a military structure, a fleet admiral, a vice admiral, and a head of financial operations. Andrew Mwangura, director of the East African Seafarers' Assistance Program, says, "They are the best organised. They have . . . training, plenty of weapons and boats, and excellent communications."[64]

Experts estimate that there are about one thousand Somali pirates in total who work the area. Most are twenty to thirty-five years old and fall into three main categories according to their background and experience. The majority are former fishermen and are considered important to operations because of their knowledge of boats and the sea. Others are ex-military men who are able and willing to attack and disable victims so a ship can be hijacked. The last group are the technical experts who operate equipment such as Global Positioning System, or GPS, devices to navigate across the water.

Rapid and Determined

When it comes to choosing their victims, the Somali pirates are not particular about whom they attack. Commercial ships are favored because they are slower and their cargo is worth millions of dollars, but even cruise ships and privately owned tourist vessels can be hit. Author and sailing enthusiast Jamie Furlong writes, "Pirates are after the big ships, but if they are unsuccessful they'll begin to run out of supplies and will therefore have no hesitation in taking on a sail boat or fishing boat in order to replenish their stocks of food and water."[65]

Attacks can come at any time of the day and are usually made in multiple small motorboats. These boats set out from a "mother ship" where the pirates live between attacks. A mother ship is a larger vessel, sometimes a pirated merchant ship, that is used as a floating base of operations. It can hold large stores of munitions and supplies and is more stable in bad weather than the small motorboats. This allows pirates to go farther from shore and attack at any time of the year. In 2011 authorities determined that up to eight mother ships were stationed off the coast of Somalia, providing protection for pirates and a place to hold hostages.

When making an attack, the pirates approach rapidly from multiple directions. They usually carry automatic weapons such as AK-47s and reloadable, shoulder-fired rocket/grenade launchers such as the RPG-7 to intimidate the unarmed ship's crew into slowing down to allow boarding. In the confusion that is created, long, lightweight ladders are used to climb aboard so that pirates can take control of the vessel and steer it into a pirate-friendly port.

A Somali pirate mother ship tows two speedboats that will be used to attack ships in the Gulf of Aden. The mother ships hold supplies, fuel, and ammunition, which allows the pirates to operate far from port.

Pirate Alley and Beyond

Pirate attacks are a regular occurrence in the waters off Somalia. The Gulf of Aden has even been nicknamed Pirate Alley because of them. Some 111 ships were accosted by Somali pirates in 2008, 214 in 2009, and 445 in 2010. Recently, the pirates began increasing their range and have started targeting ships as far south as Madagascar. They are also attacking ships in the eastern Arabian Sea closer to India. On December 5, 2010, for instance, a Bangladeshi merchant ship, the *Jahan Moni,* was hijacked 300 nautical miles (345 miles, or 555km) from the east coast of India. In April 2010 the fishing trawler *Prantalay 14* was captured by Somali pirates and was stationed about 516 nautical miles (594 miles, or 956km) off India's west coast, where it was used as a mother ship. Experts believe that by attacking farther from Somalia, the pirates are trying to avoid international naval vessels that patrol the waters off the Horn of Africa.

Not every pirate attack is successful. Somali pirates have targeted hundreds of vessels, with only a fraction of the attempts resulting in a successful hijacking. In the first part of 2009, for instance, there were twenty-one successful hijackings out of seventy-nine attempts.

Whether successful or not, every attempt is dangerous for victims. All face the possibility of death when their ship is being surrounded and boarded. If held hostage, the physical hardships that victims endure are heightened by fear and uncertainty. While many hostages survive their ordeal, the deaths of Jean and Scott Adam, Robert Riggle, and Phyllis Macay (who were killed after pirates boarded their yacht, the *Quest*) in 2011 prove that piracy is still a deadly threat.

The victims are not the only ones who face danger. A Somali pirate's career is a perilous one. There is the risk of retaliation from ships' crews or navy vessels that respond to calls for help. Pirates also deal with bad weather and accidents. Every week, men and equipment are lost at sea. For instance, the drowned body of one of the men who helped seize the *Sirius Star* in 2009 later washed ashore with his share of the ransom still on his body. Nevertheless, the pirates continue to attack. A young Somali known as Mohammed says, "Let the anti-piracy navies continue their search for us. We have no worries because our motto for the job is 'do or die.'"[66]

Big Money, Big Rewards

Like pirates of old, modern pirates are looking for treasure, and Somali pirates have discovered that big money can be made by holding commercial ships and their crews for ransom. Owners of one Chinese ship that was captured off Somalia in 2009 paid $4 million for its release. The Greek-owned *Maran Centaurus,* carrying $140 million worth of crude oil in 2009, was released in January 2010 after a ransom of between $5.5 million and $7 million was paid. Although the ransoms are large, the amounts are small in comparison to the value of the ships and the cargoes, so companies are willing to pay rather than risk losing everything. At least 26 hijacked ships and 532 hostages remain under pirate control as of 2011. Ransoms totaling $58 million were paid to pirates in 2009. Another $238 million was paid in 2010.

In addition to ships and their crews, private individuals are held for ransom. Families on small yachts are taken and held on their own ships, on ships that had previously been pirated, or, in the case of Paul and Rachel Chandler of England, in isolated bush camps on land. The Chandlers were captured on their 38-foot (11.6m) sailboat off the Seychelles on October 23, 2009. They were released on November 14, 2010, after a reported $800,000 was paid. The five members of the Danish Jan Quist Johansen family who were hijacked on their 43-foot (13m) sailboat while approaching the Horn of Africa on February 28, 2011, were held in captivity for more than six months while authorities negotiated with pirates who demanded $5 million and warned that any attempt at rescue could result in the hostages' deaths. Authorities felt that the killings aboard the *Quest* in February 2011 supported the use of force against the pirates holding the Johansen family, but after careful negotiations, a ransom of $3 million was agreed upon, and the Johansen family was released in September.

Released by Somali pirates after a reported eight hundred thousand dollars ransom was paid, Paul and Rachel Chandler recount their experience as captives.

Pirate Havens

While waiting for ransoms to be paid, the pirates often return to towns where they are relatively safe from pursuit. In the past, Somali ports like Eyl, Bossaso, and Garad have been pirate havens, but the Puntland government has taken steps to make arrests there, causing pirates to move elsewhere. "Residents and the Puntland administration forced the pirates to vacate the shores of Garad district," says businessman Abdikadir Yusuf Ali. "Now, there is not a single ship anchored off the shores of the district. All 13 ships that were here have been relocated."[67]

Other pirate strongholds remain, however. One is Harardhere, a small coastal village with dusty streets and boxy buildings. Pirated ships that are being held for ransom are anchored offshore. People who supply provisions to the hundreds of victims onboard these ships live in Harardhere, and pirates have created a "stock exchange" to manage their piracy business. Those who want to invest contribute money and then get a share of the proceeds when a ransom is paid. "We started with 15 'maritime companies' and now we are hosting 72. Ten of them have so far been successful at hijacking," Mohammed says. "The shares are open to all and everybody can take part, whether personally at sea or on land by providing cash, weapons or useful materials . . . we've made piracy a community activity."[68]

In 2011 religious extremists attacked Harardhere, demanding a portion of the pirates' takings. After this event many of the outlaws moved north to Hobyo, another pirate stronghold. Ships are now anchored offshore there, and ten-year-old boys with automatic weapons patrol the streets, on the lookout for strangers who may be extremists or authorities. The pirate presence is everywhere in Hobyo, and even villagers who are not involved in piracy appreciate how it helps the town; the pirates have set up a form of social security for those in need. The town's car dealer, who makes his living selling expensive cars to pirates after they receive a large ransom, points out, "They have allocated $100,000 to help those who are outside their business and not working."[69]

Dividing the Money

When ransoms are agreed upon, they are often paid in dollars or euros and are delivered in sturdy sacks or waterproof cases. Delivery can be by helicopter drop, by boat, or even by parachute. The latter happened in January 2009 when $3 million in cash was paid to pirates that hijacked the supertanker *Sirius Star.*

Once the ransom is paid, the pirates use sophisticated currency-counting

A hijacked French yacht lies at anchor off the coast of Puntland, Somalia. The pirates have numerous ports in Somalia from which they operate.

"Good Pirate Weather"

The crew of the Sirius Star *had no idea they were in danger as they sailed off the coast of Kenya in late 2008. When a pirate attack came, it took everyone by surprise, as journalist Auslan Cramb writes in "Sailor Tells of the Moment Pirates Captured the Sirius Star":*

James Grady, 53, was second officer on the oil tanker when men armed with machine guns and rocket-propelled grenades boarded the vessel on November 15 [2008]. ... He said the crew had been talking about the weather when two speedboats appeared. The crew of the 1,000ft [304.8m] Saudi supertanker were 500 miles [804.6km] off Kenya at the time and used fire hoses in a bid to deter the pirates. But they were forced to allow them on board when the pirates began firing in the air and threw a rope ladder with a hook on to the deck.

Mr. Grady told ITV News [in England] . . . : "We thought we were on a safe part of the ocean, in fact that morning everyone commented on how beautiful the weather was, good pirate weather as we found out."

Auslan Cramb. "Sailor Tells of the Moment Pirates Captured the Sirius Star." *Telegraph*, January 29, 2009. www.telegraph.co.uk/news/worldnews/africaandindianocean/somalia/4389151/Sailor-tells-of-the-moment-pirates-captured-the-Sirius-Star.html.

machines to tally totals and check for counterfeit bills. Then they divide up the money. "Generally, roughly 30 percent of the ransom goes to the investors, 20 percent goes to the government officials and port officials or even Islamists who guard the boat while negotiations are going on,"[70] says J. Peter Pham, an expert on Somali pirate financing at James Madison University in Harrisburg, Virginia. The remaining 50 percent goes to the pirates themselves, with those who actually board the ship getting a cut that ranges from $10,000 to $20,000. In Somalia the average income is $500 annually, so the payoff is worth the risk. Pirate Salah Ali Samatar says, "Is there any Somali who can earn $1 million for any business? We get millions of dollars easily for one attack."[71] The money is often used to buy new cell phones and cars, build large houses, and pay for extravagant lifestyles.

Dividing the spoils is just as dangerous as any other part of the operation, however. The crew is joined by shopkeepers from the shore who have been providing for the hostages and want to be paid. Arguments and fights often break out. Hostages are often caught in the middle of a chaotic situation. Captain Andrey Nozhkin of the Danish-owned merchant ship the *CEC Future* was captured by pirates in November 2008. He recalls the day the ship's ransom was paid in January 2009. "Those accused of trying to take too much had their hands slammed in doors as a punishment. Then some of the pirates started shooting, some were fighting with knives. Then other boats started arriving trying to get on board and people on the boat began shooting at them."[72]

Despite such disorganization, pirates have proved difficult to eradicate in the twenty-first century. Technology and improved communication systems should make catching them easier, but barriers still hamper capture and prosecution. Nevertheless, more effort is being made as the problem worsens and touches virtually every country in the world. Vice Admiral Mike Fox, commander of U.S. Naval Forces Central Command in the Middle East, says:

> The piracy issue requires a mosaic of different people working together—from creating the rule of law ashore in Somalia, industry leaders using best management practices, the military to patrol, disrupt and deter the pirates, and finally we need an appropriate legal "finish," so that when we catch people in the act, they're able to be taken to justice. It's an international problem and it's going to take an international cooperative solution.[73]

Chapter Six

Controlling Piracy

The countries and governments that have tried to fight piracy have learned that there is no easy way to bring the problem to an end. Whether in ancient times or modern days, pirates operate in places where conditions favor lawlessness rather than law and order. Author Peter Earle notes that the obstacles to catching them have been similar throughout time:

> The extermination of pirates [in the Golden Age] . . . posed a host of problems. . . . These were problems of diplomacy, law and public relations, manpower and resources, intelligence, strategy and tactics, and perhaps above all, motivation and will. Until states were absolutely determined to eradicate piracy and were prepared to devote considerably increased numbers of ships and men to such a policy, little would be achieved.[74]

Despite the obstacles to defeating piracy, authorities have tried many methods to deter the practice—from pardons and punishments to expanding international naval patrols and adopting high-technology defense systems. These tactics have not always been successful, and some experts have begun to look at how conditions of poverty within a country or region may motivate pirates to steal. International relations analyst Mhairi Laing points out that "by encouraging economic growth and stability in [a] country, those pushed to piracy, as a way of navigating the economic shortfalls on land, might be able to find alternative forms of lawful employment."[75] Perhaps this approach may eventually be combined with standard antipiracy activities in the fight to eliminate piracy.

Pardons

In early times officials tried a two-pronged approach to end piracy. First they offered an act of pardon—forgiveness of any crimes that had been committed. That encouraged pirates to give up their lawless ways, return home, and lead honest lives. Pardoning was tried by everyone from Emperor Jiaqing of China to King George I of Britain. King James I of England was the first to offer pardons.

Barbary corsair Captain Richard Bishop was the first notable pirate to accept such a pardon in 1611. Bishop decided he "would rather die a poor laborer in mine own county than be the richest pirate in the world,"[76] but he was in fact able to keep his illegally gotten plunder, buy a mansion, and settle down in England. Like him, Barbary corsair Henry Mainwaring was also granted a royal pardon in 1616 and returned to England after two years of piracy. He went on to lead such an honorable life that he was later knighted, elected to Parliament, and appointed a vice admiral of the Royal Navy.

Pirates were offered pardons during the Golden Age, too, but many who

King James I of England was the first to offer pirates pardons for their transgressions. Pardoning pirates soon became standard practice.

accepted them soon went back to pirating. In 1718 privateer turned pirate hunter Woodes Rogers wrote that former pirates in the Caribbean had an "itching desire to return to their former vile course of life."[77] A report from New York that same year stated that "the greatest part of them who surrendered themselves . . . are roving again."[78]

Hanging in Chains

At the same time that governments offered pardons, they punished those they caught so that other seamen would know that the price of piracy was a shameful death. Public hanging was common at the time, so most pirates were hanged, with hundreds of people turning out to view the spectacle.

Prior to each execution, much effort was made to impress the audience with how evil the pirates were. Prayers and psalms were read as pirates were led to the gallows in hopes that they would express sorrow for their crimes. Some did. For instance, Jamaican pirate John Brown confessed, "I have been guilty of all the sins in the world! I know not where to begin. I may begin with gaming! . . . Gaming led on to drinking; and drinking to lying, and swearing and cursing, and all that is bad; and so to thieving; and to this!"[79] Others stubbornly showed no remorse, like pirate William Lewis, who demanded that the onlookers share a drink with him before he died.

Even after death the punishment continued. Bodies were usually covered

A Royal Proclamation

On September 5, 1718, King George I of England issued a proclamation pardoning all pirates who would turn themselves in. The move, coupled with strict punishment of offenders who remained on the run, was designed to suppress piracy. The proclamation reads:

We do hereby Promise and Declare, That in case any of the said Pirates shall, on or before the Fifth day of September, in the Year of our Lord One thousand seven hundred and eighteen, Surrender him or themselves to One of Our Principal Secretaries of State in Great Britain or Ireland, or to any Governor or Deputy-Governor of any of Our Plantations or Dominions beyond the Seas, every such Pirate and Pirates, so Surrendering him or themselves, as aforesaid, shall have Our Gracious Pardon of and for such his or their Piracy or Piracies.

Quoted in Internet Archive. "A Proclamation for Suppressing of Pirates." www.archive.org/stream/royal proclamations12brigrich/royalproclamations12brigrich_djvu.txt.

Pirate executions were brutal affairs. This sixteenth-century woodcut depicts the execution of pirate Klaus Stoertebeker and his crew of seventy men by beheading. Their heads were then displayed to the public.

in tar, then locked into chains and iron cages and hoisted high into the air. There they hung until the flesh rotted off the bones. This could take as long as two years. The bodies of pirates William Kidd and Edward Teach were treated in this manner. After Blackbeard's death, he was beheaded and his head was hung on the prow of pirate hunter Robert Maynard's ship. When the ship returned to the port of Hampton, Virginia, the head was placed on a stake near the mouth of the nearby river as a grim deterrent to others who might consider piracy as a career. Author George Humphrey Yetter writes, "Blackbeard's skull hung for many years from a pole at the confluence [meeting of] of the Hampton and James rivers. The site is still known as Blackbeard's Point."[80]

Early Pirate Hunters

Pirates were caught because of the tireless efforts of men who often spent months or years at sea, hunting them down. One of the first recorded pirate hunters was Pompey, a friend of Julius Caesar's as well as a military and political leader in Rome in the first century B.C. The problem of piracy was so great in the Mediterranean that he was given almost the entire contents of the Roman treasury to build a fleet of five hundred ships and raise an army of 120,000 men. With this fleet Pompey effectively removed all piracy from the area in less than a year. According to the Roman writer Cicero, "Pompey made his preparations for the war at the end of the winter, entered upon it at the commencement of spring, and finished it in the middle of the summer."[81]

There were many pirate hunters, but most gained fame only when they caught a notorious pirate. In 1718, for instance, colonial leader William Rhett led a naval expedition against Stede Bonnet, the Gentleman Pirate, and captured him off Cape Fear, North Carolina. That same year Maynard became a household name when he killed Blackbeard off the coast of North Carolina. In 1722 British naval commander Chaloner Ogle defeated Bartholomew Roberts's pirate fleet off the coast of West Africa, killing the pirate captain and capturing over 250 of his men. Jonathan Barnet captured Calico Jack Rackham and his crew while they were at anchor in Dry Harbor Bay in Jamaica in October 1720.

Woodes Rogers, English sea captain, privateer, and the first royal governor of the Bahamas, was perhaps the most renowned pirate hunter. Rogers accepted the task of bringing law to the Bahamas in 1718 and began by offering pardons to those pirates who wanted to turn themselves in. At the same time, he captured and made examples of those who chose to fight. His efforts led to the public hanging of eight pirates. One of those, Thomas Morris, admitted as he climbed the gallows, "We have a good governor, but a harsh one."[82]

Mosquito Fleets

American commodore David Porter was a unique pirate hunter in that he was assigned to bring down three different sets of the outlaws at three different times in his career. He initially took part in antipiracy activities during the First Barbary War when he was first lieutenant on the navy ship USS *Philadelphia*. When it ran aground in Tripoli harbor in October 1803, he was among those captured and held prisoner until the end of the war in 1805. In 1808, after assuming command of all naval forces in the New Orleans area, Porter found him-

Fate of the Pirates

"Of the fifty-five pirate captains of this period whose fate has been determined . . . twelve surrendered and lived out their lives in varying degrees of comfort or destitution, one retired in poverty to Madagascar, six were killed in action, four drowned in shipwrecks, four were shot by their own men, one shot himself, and one was set adrift in his own boat, never to be heard from again. The remaining twenty-six were hanged."

Peter Earle. *The Pirate Wars*. New York: Thomas Dunne, 2003, p. 206.

self fighting English, French, and Spanish pirates who operated in the area. He successfully captured three French ships but discovered, due to local corruption and political complications, that he did not have support to continue the work. He was reassigned to a new post in 1810.

In 1822 Porter took on his third antipiracy assignment. He was ordered to lead a navy squadron to crack down on pirates that were attacking American ships in the Caribbean. To carry out the task, Porter was given sixteen ships, along with five barges that were shallow enough to pursue pirate vessels into coves and harbors. The barges had names like *Gnat, Midge, Mosquito,* and *Sandfly*. They became the first of what are today called Mosquito Fleets—fast-moving and maneuverable small warships such as torpedo and patrol cutters. One of Porter's first successes was the killing of Cuban pirate Diabolito (Little Devil) in 1823.

Porter was so determined and successful in restoring safe maritime trade that by 1825 piracy had virtually ceased to exist in American and Caribbean waters. He was able to state proudly, "At present I have no knowledge of the existence of any piratical establishment, vessels, or boats, or of a pirate afloat in the West Indies or Gulf of Mexico. They have all been burned, taken, destroyed, or driven to the shore."[83]

The Value of Naval Support

As the case of Porter and his squadron indicated, having access to larger navies was a great help to pirate hunters. And governments did not just add more ships to their navies as time passed, they also built large numbers of smaller, faster ships that were helpful in pursuing pirates. Several of these small naval vessels were often used as protectors for a group, or convoy, of merchant vessels that traveled together, creating a stronger presence as they passed down the Atlantic Seaboard of Europe, throughout the Mediterranean, and over to America and the West Indies.

In addition to being used as escorts, naval ships were often permanently stationed in regions that pirates frequented, so they could be at hand should they be needed to ward off an attack. The presence of these vessels, coupled with honest officials, went a long way to eradicate pirate havens. Today the combination is still proving valuable in suppressing piracy in the world. International Maritime Bureau (IMB) director Mukundan stated in 2010, "Positive and robust action by the navies against mother ships, pirate skiffs and pirate action groups has been vital to keeping the attacks under control and must be sustained."[84]

Modern Piracy Laws

When piracy again became a significant risk for ships in the 1980s, some countries had not thought of the problem for decades. Some discovered they did not even have established piracy laws. As pirate activity swelled and began to affect international shipping lanes, action and cooperation between governments lagged. To make matters worse, shipping companies hesitated

No Neutral Parties

Even back in the 1800s experts knew that fighting piracy had to be a worldwide effort. Secretary of the Navy Smith Thompson said as much to David Porter when Porter was serving as commander of the West India squadron in February 1823.

Pirates are considered, by the law of all nations, the enemies of the human race. It is the duty of all nations to put them down. . . . The nation that makes the greatest exertions to suppress such banditi, has the greatest merit. In making such exertion, it has the right to the aid of every other power, to the extent of its means, and to the enjoyment, under its sanction, of all its rights in the pursuit of the object. In the case of belligerents [hostile individuals] where the army of one party enters the territory of a neutral power, the army of the other has a right to follow it there. In the case of pirates, the right of the armed force of one power to follow them into the territory of another, is more complete. In regard to pirates there is no neutral party.

Quoted in David Dixon Porter. *Memoir of Commodore David Porter; of the United States Navy*. Albany, NY: Munsell, 1875, pp. 278–280.

U.S. naval officer David Porter was assigned to hunt pirates three separate times during his career. By 1825 piracy in U.S. waters and the Caribbean had been virtually wiped out.

to report pirate attacks because it was time-consuming, led to delays that cost thousands of dollars a day, and caused insurance costs to rise.

Those who wanted to do something were hampered by confusion over how piracy was legally defined. There was no consistency worldwide, and that sometimes provided loopholes for pirates to escape capture and punishment. For instance, the IMB, a nonprofit organization formed in 1981 to fight all kinds of maritime crime, defined piracy as "an act of boarding (or attempted boarding) with the intent to commit theft or any other crime and with the intent or capability to use force in furtherance of that act."[85]

On the other hand, the United Nations Convention on the Law of the Sea (UNCLOS) of 1982 stated that maritime piracy was any act of violence committed for private reasons by the crew of one ship against another on the high seas. The term *high seas* was significant, because that meant that according to the United Nations, pirate attacks within territorial waters—within 12 miles (19.3km) of a country's coastline—were not classified as piracy. Thus, in some cases pirates who operated within or escaped into a country's territorial waters (as is the case in the Strait of Malacca) could not be pursued by officials from another country. If the pirates fled into the waters of a country like Somalia, which did not have the will or the means to go after its own pirates within its own territorial waters, they were able to escape.

Personal Protection

Without strong protection from authorities, those who sailed through pirate-infested waters in the early twenty-first century were on their own when it came to defending themselves. A group of international shipping and trading organizations as well as the European Union, North Atlantic Treaty Organization (NATO), and the IMB soon compiled and published a handbook that became the authoritative guide for those who needed to protect themselves. The handbook is now in its third printing and is titled *Best Management Practices to Deter Piracy off the Coast of Somalia and in the Arabian Sea Area* (*BMP3*).

BMP3 advises that, as a first step, ships should let authorities know they are sailing through pirate-infested waters. They should then proceed through the area as quickly as possible. Crews should be continually on the lookout for pirates, using binoculars and night goggles. They should recognize potential threats, particularly small boats filled with many armed men, and take immediate steps, including calling for naval support. The ship should be fitted with a distinctive pirate alarm, and safe areas should be created where the crew can retreat in the event pirates get on board.

To make it harder for pirates to board, ships' decks should be ringed with coils of razor wire, and fire hoses or other water systems should be installed to spray powerful jets or walls of water over the sides. The water can be seawater, hot water, or even electrically charged water. Spraying slippery foam on decks and over the sides is another option to hinder boarding.

High-Tech Security

While small companies or independent vessels can only afford basic antipiracy measures, larger companies have begun equipping their ships with helicopters that patrol the waters where pirate activity has been reported. Some equip their ships with antipiracy weaponry such as sonic devices that send a powerful sound wave out to a directed target, bursting eardrums and causing pirates to become disoriented enough to drop their weapons. The U.S. Navy is also testing a high-energy laser that could be aimed over long distances at pirates' vessels and could set the engines on fire.

Other shipping companies have begun hiring private security companies such as Anti Piracy Maritime Security Solutions, Espada Logistics and Security Group to guard their ships. These companies offer antipiracy training for crew members and provide onboard protection from a ship's point of departure to its point of destination. That protection includes guards

Spanish trainees are instructed in maritime antipiracy operations at a training facility in Israel. Many shipping companies are turning to onboard protection for their vessels.

carrying weapons, something that commercial crews are not allowed to do.

The use of weapons on ships is controversial because shipowners do not want to risk firefights that will damage goods and expose their companies to liability suits. Attorney Stephen Askins says, "Most industry bodies and ship-owners are against them. But no ship with an armed guard has been hijacked, so there are those—particularly those who have had hijacked ships—who think they are necessary."[86] The alternatives to using weapons—being hijacked or avoiding the Indian Ocean completely—are just as controversial, especially because the latter would significantly slow and damage world trade.

Coordinating Attempts to Fight Piracy

Although it took time, by 2009 modern piracy was recognized as a global problem, and different nations began to come together to help curb attacks. For instance, the Combined Task Force 151 (CTF-151) is an antipiracy task force that is part of the U.S.-led Combined Maritime Forces (CMF), a multinational naval partnership that promotes security, stability, and prosperity in the Middle East. CMF is made up of more than twenty countries, including the United States, Canada, South Korea, France, and the United Kingdom. Members contribute intelligence personnel, surgical teams, and helicopter squadrons, among other things. Vice Admiral Bill Gortney, CMF commander in 2009, noted, "The problem of piracy is and continues to be a problem that begins ashore and is an international problem that requires an international solution. We believe the establishment of CTF-151 is a significant step in the right direction."[87]

The European Union is another multinational group that is playing a significant role in combating piracy off the coast of Somalia. Its Operation Atalanta (formally European Union Naval Force Somalia) works to protect vessels of the World Food Programme (WFP) that deliver food aid to displaced persons in Somalia. The operation also protects vulnerable vessels cruising off the Somali coast from piracy and armed robbery. It is made up of five to ten naval ships, one or two auxiliary ships, and two to four reconnaissance aircraft.

The NATO task force Operation Ocean Shield is a third international antipiracy group. Beginning in 2008 as Operation Allied Protector, its NATO member countries aim to safeguard ships from pirates in the Indian Ocean and Gulf of Aden and assist countries in the region to develop their own antipiracy capabilities. An April 2011 operation, when a Turkish warship captured a pirate mother ship filled with weapons, marked a significant success for the Ocean Shield operation. NATO commander Michiel Hijmans stated afterward, "This swift action immediately after the attack on the merchant vessel shows the importance of good cooperation between the merchant community, CMF and NATO forces in counter piracy. Another pirate action group has been taken from the sea."[88]

A French frigate escorts a World Food Programme ship in Somali waters. From NATO to the European Union to China, world powers are coordinating massive antipiracy operations.

Prosecuting Pirates

Once pirates are caught, prosecuting them can be difficult. Because the Somali government does not have the desire or the means to deal with all cases of piracy, the country involved in capturing the outlaws usually takes responsibility for imprisoning them and bringing them to trial. The captor country also has to take responsibility for the costs of the pirate's imprisonment and trial. With trials scheduled in a variety of places, prosecutors sometimes spend much time and money arranging transportation for witnesses and finding translators for the pirates.

Despite the difficulties, some piracy trials have taken place. Eighteen pirates have been convicted in Kenya since 2008, and over one hundred suspects there are awaiting trial. In May 2010 a Yemeni court sentenced six Somali pirates to death and jailed six others for ten years each for the 2009 hijacking of a Yemeni oil tanker that left one crew member dead. The first trial by a Western country opened in Netherlands in May 2010. The five defendants were arrested in the Gulf of Aden in January 2009 while allegedly preparing to board the cargo ship *Samanyolu*, registered in the Dutch Antilles. The pirates were found guilty and sentenced to five years in prison.

The United States put its first captured pirates on trial in a federal court in Virginia in November 2010. Five Somalis were found guilty of attacking the USS *Nicholas* while it was on patrol off the Somali coast in April 2010. They were given life sentences. Then in February 2011 a New York federal court sentenced Somali pirate Abdiwali Abdiqadir Muse to thirty-three years in prison for seizing the *Maersk Alabama* and kidnapping its captain. In March 2011 a federal grand jury indicted thirteen suspected pirates from Somalia and one from Yemen in the February hijacking of the *Quest* that left Jean Adam, Scott Adam, Robert Riggle, and Phyllis Macay dead. The men face piracy, kidnapping, and firearms charges stemming from their efforts to hold the Americans for ransom. FBI agent Janice K. Fedarcyk stated, "Today's charges should send a clear message to those who attempt to engage in piracy against Americans or American vessels—even on the open ocean, you are not beyond the reach of American justice."[89]

A Glimmer of Hope

Controlling pirates through international cooperation, persistence, and

This courtroom sketch artist's drawing depicts five Somali pirates on trial for their attack on the USS Nicholas *in April 2010. They were convicted in the first piracy trial in the United States in over two hundred years.*

prosecution is possible, as efforts in the Strait of Malacca demonstrate. In 2006 fourteen countries, including Japan, China, South Korea, India, Thailand, and the Philippines, joined forces in a network called the Regional Cooperation Agreement on Combating Piracy and Armed Robbery Against Ships in Asia (ReCAAP). Singapore Transport Ministry's Permanent Secretary, Brigadier General Choi Shing Kwok, says, "Piracy is a transnational problem and this is the first time an international body has been set up to deal solely with the problem of piracy in Asia."[90] Although Indonesia and Malaysia are not ReCAAP members, they have joint antipiracy initiatives with Singapore and formed the Malacca Strait Patrols in 2004. It works to increase security and decrease attacks in the strait. The countries use technology, air and marine patrols, and share information so that they can be consistent in their efforts.

These efforts seem to have been successful. The IMB has found that the number of actual and attempted piracy attacks in the Strait of Malacca dropped from eleven in 2006 to two in 2010. Journalist Michael Schuman says, "The case of Malacca gives at least a glimmer of hope that the piracy problem in Africa can also be tackled. The success in the strait clearly shows how committed and carefully orchestrated naval action can combat pirates."[91]

Just as in the past, however, when pirates are pushed out of one area, they often move to another. The focus of piracy in Asia has shifted eastward into the South China Sea, which recorded only one pirate attack in 2006 but more than thirty in 2010. There has been an increase in Somali pirate attacks off the coast of India, too, as more naval ships threaten them off the Horn of Africa.

The figures are proof that patrolling waters and deterring attacks are just part of the solution. Experts point out that when the poor have nowhere to turn and when governments are unstable or uncaring, individuals are prone to break the law. Therefore, it is likely that piracy will continue to be a problem in the modern world, just as it had been in earlier times. Daring individuals will continue to be tempted by the thought of easy riches. The vast expanse of water on which they operate will make it difficult for authorities to make captures. Nevertheless, dedicated men and women will continue to fight the crimes, try to bring offenders to justice, and work to convict them, just as they always have. "I think we have to make the punishment so severe that they go with options other than heading to sea," says FBI investigator Kevin P. Couglin, a modern-day pirate fighter. "Obviously the more pirates we catch, the safer the waters are going to be."[92]

Notes

Introduction: Fact and Fantasy

1. Quoted in MSNBC.com. "Sailor Held by Somali Pirates a 'True Adventurist.'" February 21, 2011. www.msnbc.msn.com/id/41672888/ns/world_news-africa.
2. Charlotte Sector. "Danger Adrift: Modern-Day Pirates Threaten More than the High Seas." ABC News, November 14, 2005. http://abcnews.go.com/International/story?id=1300344.
3. Peter Earle. *The Pirate Wars*. New York: Thomas Dunne, 2003, p. 7.
4. Quoted in Earle. *The Pirate Wars*, p. 9.
5. Edward E. Leslie. *Desperate Journeys, Abandoned Souls: True Stories of Castaways and Other Survivors*. New York: Houghton Mifflin, 1988, p. 87.
6. Angus Konstam. *Piracy: The Complete History*. New York: Osprey, 2008, p. 303.

Chapter One: The Barbary Pirates

7. Cindy Vallar. "When Is a Pirate Not a Pirate?" Pirates and Privateers. www.cindyvallar.com/definitions.html.
8. Ellen Churchill Semple. "Pirate Coasts of the Mediterranean Sea." *Geographical Review*, August 1916, p. 135.
9. Earle. *The Pirate Wars*, p. 43.
10. Earle. *The Pirate Wars*, p. 49.
11. Quoted in Konstam. *Piracy*, p. 91.
12. Earle. *The Pirate Wars*, p. 44.
13. Earle. *The Pirate Wars*, p. 46.
14. Konstam. *Piracy*, p. 83.
15. Stanley Lane-Poole and James Douglas Jerrold Kelley. *The Story of the Barbary Corsairs*. New York: Putnam, 1890, p. 52.
16. Lane-Poole and Kelley. *The Barbary Corsairs*, pp. 53–54.
17. Lane-Poole and Kelley. *The Barbary Corsairs*, p. 59.
18. Quoted in Leslie Hotson. "Pirates in Parchment." *Atlantic Monthly*, August 1927. www.theatlantic.com/past/docs/issues/27aug/hotson.htm.
19. Lane-Poole and Kelley. *The Barbary Corsairs*, p. 229.
20. Avalon Project, Yale Law School. "Thomas Jefferson, First Annual Message to Congress." December 8, 1801. http://avalon.law.yale.edu/19th_century/jeffmes1.asp.
21. Konstam. *Piracy*, p. 94.
22. Earle. *The Pirate Wars*, p. 90.

Chapter Two: Piracy in the Caribbean

23. Rene Chartrand, *The Spanish Main, 1492–1800*. New York: Osprey, 2006, p. 18.
24. Quoted in Konstam. *Piracy*, p. 61.

25. Konstam. *Piracy*, p. 101.
26. Quoted in Captain Charles Johnson. *A General History of the Pyrates*. London: Warner, 1724, pp. 272–273.
27. Konstam. *Piracy*, p. 104.
28. Earle. *The Pirate Wars*, p. 94.
29. Konstam. *Piracy*, p. 115.
30. Quoted in Stephen Talty. *Empire of the Blue Water*. New York: Crown, 2007, pp. 139–140.
31. Quoted in Larry Gragg. "The Port Royal Earthquake." *History Today*, September 2000, p. 30.
32. Konstam. *Piracy*, p. 251.
33. Quoted in Konstam. *Piracy*, p. 253.
34. Earle. *The Pirate Wars*, p. 120.

Chapter Three: The Pirate Life

35. David Cordingly. *Under the Black Flag: The Romance and the Reality of Life Among the Pirates*. New York: Random House, 1995, p. xx.
36. Earle. *The Pirate Wars*, p. 101.
37. Quoted in Johnson. *A General History of the Pyrates*, p. 232.
38. Quoted in Earle. *The Pirate Wars*, p. 172.
39. Quoted in Johnson. *A General History of the Pyrates*, p. 77.
40. Quoted in Konstam. *Piracy*, p. 185.
41. Johnson. *A General History of the Pyrates*, p. 161.
42. Quoted in Konstam. *Piracy*, p. 185.
43. Earle. *The Pirate Wars*, p. 105.
44. Quoted in Cordingly. *Under the Black Flag*, p. 10.
45. Quoted in Cordingly. *Under the Black Flag*, p. 117.
46. Quoted in Konstam. *Piracy*, p. 118.
47. Quoted in Konstam. *Piracy*, p. 216.
48. Johnson. *A General History of the Pyrates*, p. 390.
49. Johnson. *A General History of the Pyrates*, pp. 87–88.
50. George Francis Dow and John Henry Edmonds. *The Pirates of the New England Coast, 1630–1730*. New York: Dover, 1996, p. 168.
51. Earle. *The Pirate Wars*, p. 206.

Chapter Four: Piracy in Asia

52. Konstam. *Piracy*, p. 288.
53. H. Warington Smyth. *Mast and Sail in Europe and Asia*. New York: Dutton, 1960, p. 397.
54. Quoted in Hindu Janajagruti Samiti. "Sarkhel Kanhoji Angre: The Admiral of the Great Maratha Navy." www.hindujagruti.org/articles/index.php?print/id:40.
55. Konstam. *Piracy*, p. 295.
56. Konstam. *Piracy*, p. 298.
57. Konstam. *Piracy*, p. 297.
58. George Wingrove Cook. *China: Being "The Times" Special Correspondence from China in the Years 1857–58*. London: Routledge, 1859, p. 68.
59. Nur Jale. "The Threat of Modern Day Piracy in Strategic Waters." *Eurasia Critic*, January 2009. www.eurasiacritic.com/articles/threat-modern-day-piracy-strategic-waters.

Chapter Five: Piracy in Modern Times

60. Quoted in Stefan Lovgren. "Modern Pirates Terrorize Seas with Guns and Grenades." *National Geographic*, July 6, 2006. news.nationalgeographic.com/news/2006/07/060706-modern-pirates.html.

61. P.P. Sivamani. "The Limos Are Here to Stay." *Naval Dispatch*, December 2005, p. 13.
62. Eric Koo. "Terror on the High Seas, Part 1." *Asia Times*, October 19, 2004. www.atimes.com/atimes/Southeast_Asia/FJ19Ae01.html.
63. Michael G. Frodl. "Hijacked Super Tanker Exposes Vulnerability of Energy Supplies." National Defense Industrial Association, March 2009. www.nationaldefensemagazine.org/archive/2009/March/Pages/HijackedSuperTankerExposesVulnerabilityofEnergySupplies.aspx.
64. Quoted in John Lichfield. "Yacht Raid Reveals Hi-Tech Somali Pirate Network." *Independent*, April 10, 2008. www.independent.co.uk/news/world/africa/yacht-raid-reveals-hitech-somali-pirate-network-807022.html.
65. Jamie Furlong. "Pirate Alley, Putting It in Perspective." Follow the Boat.com, March 9, 2010. www.followtheboat.com/2010/03/09/pirate-alley-putting-it-in-perspective.
66. Quoted in Mohamed Ahmed. "Somali Sea Gangs Lure Investors at Pirate Lair." Reuters, December 1, 2009. www.reuters.com/article/2009/12/01/us-somalia-piracy-investors-idUSTRE5B01Z920091201?pageNumber=2.
67. Quoted in Mohamed Ahmed. "Somali Pirates Quit One Puntland Base, Head South." Reuters, February 2, 2011. www.hiiraan.com/news2/2011/feb/somali_pirates_quit_one_puntland_base_head_south.aspx.
68. Quoted in Ahmed. "Somali Sea Gangs Lure Investors at Pirate Lair."
69. Quoted in Sahal Abdulle and Rob Crilly. "Somali Fishermen Opt for Piracy's Rich Pickings." *London Times*, April 7, 2009. www.timesonline.co.uk/tol/news/world/africa/article6045092.ece.
70. Quoted in Somali Directory. "Pirates, Inc.: Inside the Booming Somali Business." August 31, 2009. www.somalidirectory.net/biz/business-news/2-pirates-inc-inside-the-booming-somali-business.html.
71. Quoted in Shashank Bengali. "Forget Depp: Somali Pirates Risk All for Riches, Women." *Christian Science Monitor*, December 19, 2008. www.csmonitor.com/World/Africa/2008/1219/p25s41-woaf.html.
72. Quoted in Rob Walker. "Inside Story of Somali Pirate Attack." BBC, June 4, 2009. news.bbc.co.uk/2/hi/africa/8080098.stm.
73. Quoted in Combined Maritime Forces. "UAE Steps into the Fight Against Piracy." April 26, 2011. http://combinedmaritimeforces.com.

Chapter Six: Controlling Piracy

74. Earle. *The Pirate Wars*, p. 61.
75. Mhairi Laing. "Completing the Cycle: Ending Piracy off the Coast of Somalia." Henry Jackson Society, January 11, 2010. www.henryjacksonsociety.org/stories.asp?id=1342.
76. Quoted in Earle, *The Pirate Wars*, p. 61.
77. Quoted in Earle. *The Pirate Wars*, p. 192.

78. Quoted in Earle. *The Pirate Wars*, p. 192.
79. Quoted in Cordingly. *Under the Black Flag*, p. 239.
80. George Humphrey Yetter. "When Blackbeard Scourged the Seas." *Colonial Williamsburg Journal*, Autumn 1992, p. 28. www.history.org/Foundation/journal/blackbea.cfm.
81. Quoted in William Smith. *A Classical Dictionary of Biography, Mythology and Geography Based on Larger Dictionaries*. London: Murray, 1891, p. 603.
82. Quoted in Colin Woodard. *The Republic of Pirates: Being the True and Surprising Story of the Caribbean Pirates and the Man Who Brought Them Down*. New York: Harcourt, 2007, p. 303.
83. Quoted in Kevin M. McCarthy. *Twenty Florida Pirates*. Sarasota, FL: Pineapple, 1994, p. 69.
84. Quoted in Eileen Ng and Elaine Ganley. "Somali Pirates Seize Ship with 21 Filipinos Aboard." Fox News, April 21, 2010. www.foxnews.com/world/2010/04/21/somali-pirates-seize-ship-aboard/?test=latestnews.
85. Quoted in Maritime Terrorism Research Center. "Definitions." www.maritimeterrorism.com/definitions.
86. Quoted in Kathryn Westcott. "'Pirate' Death Puts Spotlight on 'Guns for Hire.'" BBC, March 24, 2010. http://news.bbc.co.uk/2/hi/africa/8585967.stm.
87. Quoted in Global Security.org. "New Counter-Piracy Task Force Established." January 8, 2009. www.globalsecurity.org/military/library/news/2009/01/mil-090108-nns02.htm.
88. Quoted in Allied Maritime Command Headquarters Northwood News Release. "NATO Warship Helps to Free Captured Vessel." April 26, 2011. www.manw.nato.int/pdf/Press%20Releases%202011/Press%20releases%20Jan-June%202011/SNMG2/26%2004%2011%20NATO%20News%20ReleaseNATOWarshipHelpsto%20FreeCapturedVessel.pdf.
89. Quoted in Julie Mianecki. "14 Suspected Pirates Indicted in Attack on Yacht That Left 4 Americans Dead." *Los Angeles Times*, March 11, 2011. http://articles.latimes.com/2011/mar/11/nation/la-na-pirates-indictment-20110311.
90. Quoted in T. Rajan. "14 Nation Network's Anti-Piracy Coordination Centre Opens Here." *Straits Times*, November 23, 2006. http://app.mfa.gov.sg/pr/read_content.asp?View,5914,.
91. Michael Schuman. "How to Defeat Pirates: Success in the Strait." *Time*, April 22, 2009. www.time.com/time/world/article/0,8599,1893032,00.html.
92. Quoted in Joseph Goldstein. "FBI's Man on the Pirate Beat, Seeking Confessions." *New York Times*, August 22, 2011. www.nytimes.com/2011/08/22/nyregion/fbis-man-on-the-pirate-beat-seeking-confessions.html?pagewanted=2&_r=1&ref=piracyatsea.

Glossary

articles of regulation: A contract signed by pirates when joining a ship, stating rules and shares of profits.

bey: A provincial governor in the Ottoman Empire.

buccaneer: A settler who dried the meat from wild cattle on the island of Hispaniola in the early 1600s; later, a name for *pirate* in the Caribbean.

bumboo: A mixture of rum, water, sugar, and nutmeg.

careen: To beach a ship in order to clean and repair it.

convoy: A group of vessels traveling together.

corsair: A pirate along the Barbary Coast.

doubloon: A gold coin minted by Spain or Spanish colonies; worth about seven weeks' pay for an average sailor.

***flibustier*:** A French term for a pirate during the Golden Age.

galivat: A small armed vessel with sails and oars.

galleon: A large, square-masted sailing vessel used mainly for war or commerce.

galley: A seagoing vessel propelled mainly by oars.

ghurab: An Indian warship.

International Maritime Bureau (IMB): The nonprofit organization that acts as a focal point in the fight against all types of maritime crime.

junk: A wooden sailing ship used primarily in Asia.

lantaka: A swivel cannon.

letter of marque: A document proving that a privateer was sponsored by a government to attack and loot the ships of an enemy.

maritime piracy: The robberies and/or criminal acts of violence committed on any major body of water and the land edging that water.

maroon: To put ashore and abandon on a deserted island as a form of punishment.

Mosquito Fleet: A fast-moving and maneuverable small warship such as torpedo and patrol cutters.

mother ship: A vessel used as a floating base of operations for modern pirates.

North Atlantic Treaty Organization (NATO): The military alliance made up of twenty-eight countries from North America and Europe.

pancung: A small wooden boat with an outboard motor.

pieces of eight: Spanish silver coins or old Spanish pesos equal to eight reals.

pike: A weapon made up of a sharp blade mounted on a staff.

pinnace: A light boat propelled by sails or oars.

privateer: A pirate working for a government to fight or harass enemy ships.

salmagundi: A dish that is a mixture of whatever a cook has on hand; can include chopped meat, fish, onions, eggs, and spices.

schooner: A fore-and-aft rigged sailing vessel having at least two masts.

shanty: A song sung by pirates to the rhythm of their movements while working.

sloop: A single-masted sailing boat, favored by pirates for maneuvering in shallow water.

Spanish Main: The lands taken by Spain in the 1600s, stretching from Mexico to Peru and including the Caribbean Islands.

woolding: A form of torture inflicted by passing a length of knotted cord around a man's head and then twisting the cord more tightly.

For More Information

Books

Pat Croce. *Blackbeard*. Philadelphia: Running Press Kids, 2011. The history of an authentic American villain.

Robert Louis Stevenson. *Treasure Island*. New York: Grosset and Dunlap, 1947. First published in 1883, this classic story established many of the popular perceptions about pirates.

Jane Yolen. *Sea Queens*. Watertown, MA: Charlesbridge, 2008. Covers the lives and legends surrounding a variety of female pirates, including Anne Bonny, Mary Read, and Madam Zheng.

Internet Sources

Amy Crawford. "The Gentleman Pirate." *Smithsonian*, August 1, 2007. www.smithsonianmag.com/history-archaeology/biography/pirates.html?onsite_source=relatedarticles&onsite_medium=internallink&onsite_campaign=SmithMag&onsite_content=The%20Gentleman%20Pirate.

Paul Raffaele. "The Pirate Hunters." *Smithsonian*, August 2007. www.smithsonianmag.com/people-places/pirate_main.html?onsite_source=relatedarticles&onsite_medium=internallink&onsite_campaign=SmithMag&onsite_content=The%20Pirate%20Hunters.

Abigail Tucker. "Did Archaeologists Uncover Blackbeard's Treasure?" *Smithsonian*, March 2011. www.smithsonianmag.com/history-archaeology/Did-Archaeologists-Uncover-Blackbeards-Treasure.html.

Websites

Brethren of the Coast (http://brethrencoast.com). Explores pirate facts and fiction. Includes articles on pirate flags, weapons, songs, ships, and movies.

International Maritime Bureau (IMB) Piracy Reporting Centre (www.icc-ccs.org/piracy-reporting-centre). Gives modern piracy news and statistics, maps where piracy is occurring, piracy-prone areas, and more.

Pirates and Privateers: The History of Maritime Piracy (www.cindyvallar.com/pirates.html). An excellent website that includes articles about every aspect of maritime piracy, classroom activities, and links to other literature.

Pirates Realm (www.thepiratesrealm.com). In addition to a wide range of information about pirates, this website includes a list of pirate museums that can be visited in the United States and other countries.

Index

Picture Credits

Cover: © North Wind Picture Archive/ Alamy
Anthony Njuguna/Reuters/Landov, 9
AP Images, 68
AP Images/Alba Bragoli, 87
AP Images/Alex Cave, Royal Navy, 67
AP Images/Farah Abdi Warsemeh, 72
AP Images/North Wind Picture Archives, 53
The Art Archive, 34, 39
The Art Archive/Domenica del Corriere/Gianni Dagli Orti, 60
The Art Archive/J. Baylor Roberts/NGS Image Collection, 30
Art Resource, NY, 44
Barbary Pirates Attacking A Spanish Ship (oil on canvas), Velde, Willem van de II, (1633–1707) (studio of) / Private Collection/Photo © Christie's Images/The Bridgeman Art Library International, 24
Captain Bartholomew Roberts, engraved by James Basire, 1772 (engraving), English School/Private Collection/ Peter Newark Historical Pictures/The Bridgeman Art Library International, 46
David Silverman/Getty Images, 84
© DeAgostini/SuperStock, 12
© DeA Picture Library/Art Resource, NY, 8
DeA Picture Library/De Agostini/Getty Images, 55
The disappearance of Port Royal in 1692, Howat, Andrew (20th Century)/ Private Collection/© Look and Learn The Bridgeman Art Library, 31
dpa/Landov, 73
© GL Archive/Alamy, 25, 27
Helene Seligman/AFP/Getty Images, 9
Henry Guttmann/Getty Images, 79
Hulton Archive/Getty Images, 37, 82
José Cendon/AFP/Getty Images, 86
The Library of Congress, 15
Madame Ching, legendary Chinese Pirate Queen (engraving), American School, (18th century)/Private Collection/Peter Newark Historical Pictures/The Bridgeman Art Library International, 57
Morgan at Porto Bello, from 'Buccaneers and Marooners of the Spanish Main' (coloured engraving), Pyle, Howard (1853--1911) (after)/Private Collection/Photo © Leemage/ AISA /The Bridgeman Art Library International, 32
Paul Popper/Popperfoto/Getty Images, 21
© The Print Collector/Corbis, 43
Reuters/ECPAD - Sirpa Marine--French Ministry of Defence/Landov, 70
SSPL/Getty Images, 52
© SuperStock/SuperStock, 48
Supri/Reuters/Landov, 66
Universal History Archive/Getty Images, 17, 41, 77
© Universal Images Group/SuperStock, 9
© Zainal Abd Halim/01060/Reuters/ Corbis, 64

About the Author

Diane Yancey lives in the Pacific Northwest with her husband, Michael, and their cats, Newton, Lily, and Alice. She has written more than twenty-five books for middle-grade and high school readers, including *Art Deco*, *Basketball*, and *Tracking Serial Killers*.